Genesis Analysis for Pastors

Using Science to Evaluate the Claims of the Bible

Richard Sanders

A series of messages to equip church leaders, pastors and Bible teachers to defend the authority of the first eleven chapters of Genesis as being consistent with the principles of science

Genesis Analysis for Pastors

This book is manufactured in the United States of America

Publisher: Kindle Direct Publishing
kdp.amazon.com

ISBN 9798718448283

LCCN

Bulk Orders

Quantity discounts are available on bulk purchases of this book for ministries and evangelical organizations. Discounts are also available to schools, libraries, corporations and other organizations. To learn more, send an email to contactrichardsanders@gmail.com or call (843) 290-1811.

How to contact the author

Richard Sanders is an author, public speaker and a former science teacher. He speaks on topics related to creation science and biblical apologetics. Additional resources are available to those wishing to use these messages in their own presentations, which include:

- Digital, editable copies in Microsoft Word® or PDF format are available, allowing a customer to cut-and-paste or change the written style to fit one's preferred format for sermons or lectures.
- Microsoft PowerPoint® presentations to accompany each message are also available.

To contact Mr. Sanders for a speaking engagement, interview, appearance at a vendor's booth, or to request the above resources, please send an email to contactrichardsanders@gmail.com

TABLE OF CONTENTS

All biblical quotations are from the New American Standard Version unless indicated otherwise.

FOREWORD*

The Gospel We Are Called to Preach

Many Christians are asking, "Why can't we avoid all this controversy about creation and just preach Christ?" Such a question ignores clear declarations in Scripture that Christ is our Creator. John 1: 1-3 stands out as one of the most emphatic, identifying the Word (Jesus Christ) as being present in the beginning, that He was both with God and was God, and that "All things came into being by Him, and apart from Him nothing came into being that has come into being."

The doctrine of creation as it relates to Christ is not a minor biblical principle of superficial importance. To ignore it is dangerous and is analogous to preaching "another Jesus" (2 Corinthians 11:4) when we neglect to present Christ as He truly is, along with His complete work.

To truly preach Christ in all His fullness requires that we recognize Him as the almighty Creator who spoke the universe into existence (Psalm 33: 9) and walked with Adam and Eve in the cool of the day (Genesis 3:8). It wasn't long before they sinfully rejected the Creator's rightful authority, and their separation from Him ushered in the current world of death and decay. We can (thank God) be reconciled to Him again, but it is only meaningful to preach of Christ's love and great gift of salvation when we acknowledge Him first as the offended Creator.

Jesus Christ was our Creator long before he became our Savior and coming Reconciler, and the full gospel must include all three components. The late Dr. Henry Morris II, founder of the Institute for Creation Research, eloquently made this point in one of his final public speaking engagements:

> A gospel without the creation has no foundation. A gospel without the consummation has no hope. And a gospel without the cross and empty tomb has no power. But ... if you have the *whole* thing ... then you can have a sure foundation, a blessed hope, and all power in heaven and earth – and *that's* the gospel we are called to preach!

This is the essence of this series of messages. It is not enough to "just preach Christ" if we fail to present Him in all his fullness as our Creator and coming King. We should be committed to the complete veracity of Scripture – including the truth of special and recent creation as recorded in Genesis and affirmed through scientific research.

*Adapted from Morris, H.M. IV, 2020, "The Gospel We Are Called to Preach", *Acts & Facts*, 49(4):22, Institute for Creation Research, Dallas, TX

Preface

Over the considerable number of decades of my life I have listened to thousands of pastoral messages that have been wonderful in teaching me about the Bible and how to apply it to my life, but only a handful of these have dealt with *apologetics*, which basically means giving listeners solid, logical *reasons to believe* [1 Peter 3:15]. Furthermore, with the exception of the late Dr. D. James Kennedy, virtually none of these messages dealt with defending the first eleven chapters of the book of Genesis. Ever since Charles Darwin's book *On the Origin of Species* made it "acceptable to be an atheist", a majority of scientists over the last 160 years have rejected the notion of a Creator God, turning instead to the theory of evolution as an explanation of how we came to be here.

Instead of actively opposing this trend toward materialism, secularism and humanism, church leaders have gradually succumbed to it, endeavoring to somehow fit evolution and deep time (millions of years) into the Bible with concepts like a Gap Theory, Day-Age Theory, Progressive Evolution, Theistic Evolution, etc. The media, schools and universities (even many Christian ones) indoctrinate the public that evolution has been scientifically proven and therefore cannot be questioned.

It is not surprising, then, that most pastors feel unqualified to challenge this societal trend from their pulpits. They fear losing their members if they promote the book of Genesis as historical truth in opposition to the mainstream "scientific worldview". Most pastors lack much training in the sciences, and have not had the time or opportunity to immerse themselves in the literature and research that support a creation worldview. Some have invited speakers in from creationist organizations such as Answers in Genesis, Creation Ministries International and the Institute for Creation Research, but most have chosen to simply avoid the controversy altogether and simply "preach Jesus".

Unfortunately, study after study has shown that church membership (and belief in God) is steadily declining in the western world, especially North America. Reasons given are typically something like: "I think science has disproven the Bible"; "The Bible is no longer relevant in this century"; or "My professors taught me that religions are based on myths and superstition." For many years I was in agreement with such statements until I was exposed to the counterarguments put forward by organizations like those mentioned above.

My background in science, coupled with years of applying my critical thinking skills to analyzing the competing arguments, ultimately led me to write this book of messages for pastors and Bible teachers to use in teaching the authority of God's word.

Each message is designed to be delivered in 30 to 45 minutes (a typical "sermon time" for most churches). Depending on the audience, **the presenter may wish to present the material in the Introduction as a separate message** to set the stage for the remaining messages. For digital editions of the text for copying and editing these messages as you see fit, see the author's contact page.

If you find these resources helpful, to God be the glory.

Richard Sanders

ACKNOWLEDGEMENTS

In writing this series of messages I have borrowed heavily from the book *The Genesis Account* by Dr. Jonathan Sarfati. You could even say that this is a condensed version of his nearly 800-page tome. Super-scripted page numbers in brackets are used to cite his book where it is believed a reader may want to authenticate information more thoroughly, but for the sake of readability, not every phrase borrowed from his book is cited. The reader who intends to use these messages in his or her own presentations is strongly encouraged to read Dr. Sarfati's book in its entirety, especially the chapters that parallel each message, to insure a better understanding of the material.

Other sources are cited (as necessary) by superscripted numerals referring to the Endnotes and References page. That is also where you will find the publisher and copyright information for Dr. Sarfati's book.

The careful reader will find many statements in these messages that do not cite an authoritative source. This is not intended to be a formal research paper, so if a declarative statement is generally known to the creation science community, no specific reference will be cited. However, for the skeptical reader a simple Internet search will provide much authoritative support from hundreds of articles published by accredited sources. Within the young Earth creationist community, I offer the following web sites where thousands of articles can be accessed using the word-search engines on each site:

answersingenesis.org: Largest online creationist web site hosted by Answers in Genesis
creation.com: Web site for Creation Ministries International
icr.org: Web site for the Institute for Creation Research, founded by Dr. Henry Morris II
creationresearch.org: Web site for the Creation Research Society

INTRODUCTION

Science 101: Theoretical Models Applied to Historical Science

During the past century and a half, it has become quite fashionable to deny a straightforward, literal interpretation of the Bible, and especially the first eleven chapters of the book of Genesis. Liberal theologians and many Christian leaders have adopted interpretations that are practically indistinguishable from those of skeptics, agnostics and even atheists – denying: a six-day creation; a human origin beginning with a specially created Adam and Eve; original sin leading to death and suffering; a judgment in the form of a worldwide Flood; and a divine scattering of tribes and people groups following an act of rebellion at the Tower of Babel.

These deniers have hijacked the concept of "science" in an attempt to buttress their arguments against the authority of the Bible. According to the laws of logic (upon which modern science is based), two opposing statements cannot both be true, although they could both be false. When two, *and only two*, possibilities exist, then only one statement can be true. To ascertain Truth is the overarching goal of all scientific research, but scientific research has certain limitations:

a) Scientific research can only investigate the material world. This rules out spiritual, aesthetic, metaphysical, miraculous and other-dimensional phenomena.

b) *Operational science* (also called empirical or experimental) can only investigate phenomena that are observable in the present time and that have a hypothetical explanation that can be tested experimentally, can be falsified if unsupported, and can be repeated if supported, all of which would lead to further investigation and formulation of additional hypotheses. All conclusions arrived at through operational science are tentative, but when re-affirmed many times over may eventually be accepted as a scientific theory or even as a scientific law. Throughout history many scientific theories have been discarded (e.g., caloric theory of heat, phlogiston theory of combustion, biological theory of spontaneous generation), and many have been substantially modified or revised (e.g., atomic theory, germ theory, genetic theory). To date, no scientific law has been falsified, although some may have been found to be true only within certain limits (e.g., Newton's law of universal gravitation has to be modified to account for relativistic effects).

c) *Historical science* (also called forensic science) is often invoked for phenomena that only happened in the past and are no longer happening, and/or were not (or cannot be) observed. Examples of branches of science that investigate such phenomena include archeology, paleontology, anthropology and cosmology (think Big Bang). Historical science cannot use the *scientific method* of operational science, but instead formulates *theoretical models* to describe events of the past, and then seeks evidence in the present that either supports or does not support the model. An example is the Standard Model of quantum physics that postulates invisible forces and particles and yet is able to do a fair job explaining and even predicting new discoveries.

d) Clearly if one is going look to "science" to investigate the first eleven chapters of Genesis, it can only be within the realm of *historical science*, since these events were either not observed (e.g., Creation), or only happened once and are thus non-repeatable (e.g., original sin, worldwide Flood).

Setting Up the Investigation

Since only *historical science* can be used to investigate Genesis 1-11, we must establish what *theoretical models* can be considered to have explanatory power. Using ordinary reason and logic (foundational to science), it seems there are only three possibilities:

a) The universe (heavens & earth) was created.
b) The universe (heavens & earth) came about by an uncaused event, or
c) The universe (heavens & earth) is eternal.

It would be marvelous if we could reduce these three possibilities down to two, since then we could assert that according to the laws of logic, only one of the two competing theories could be true. (We will indulge ourselves the belief that there are no other possibilities, therefore they could not both be false.) Most (but not all) scientists today who study the cosmos agree that the third option, an eternal universe, is no longer viable, although for many years it was the prevailing belief of scientists who did not accept the biblical explanation of origins (including Albert Einstein). Beginning with astronomer Edwin Hubble in the 1920's, astronomers have come to believe that the shift in the wavelength of light coming from distant galaxies toward the red end of the visible spectrum is best explained by an *expanding universe*, and that in fact the rate of that expansion is actually increasing. The deduction from this observation is profound: if the universe is expanding, then it must be expanding *from something*, in other words the universe must have had a beginning! A small minority of astronomers contend that this apparent red-shift can be explained by causes other than an expanding universe, while others acknowledge the expansion, but claim it is part of an eternal oscillating universe that has been expanding, then contracting into a "big crunch", then expanding again, forever. For the purposes of our investigation, we will discount the possibility of an eternal universe for two reasons: 1) it is a model only held by a small minority of scientists today, and 2) it cannot be investigated by either historical *or* operational science since there is no evidence supporting it, and in fact would violate the 2nd Law of Thermodynamics [97] .

So, we find ourselves left with two, and only two, competing theoretical models. We will call the first the **Creation Model** and the second the **Evolution Model**. Only one of these models can be true, since we have eliminated other possibilities. While critics will maintain that only the evolution model is "scientific", that is not true. Neither model can be investigated by operational science, since they both deal with unobservable phenomena that happened in the past, are not happening now, and are not observable by scientists in the present. However, *both* can be investigated using historical science by determining to what degree **evidence** we see today *supports*, or *fails to support*, a given model.

The Creation Model

The Law of Cause and Effect implies that no effect can be greater than its cause[97]. Since the Creation Model asserts the universe was created, then the Creator (or First Cause) cannot be part of the creation, i.e., we say the Cause is *transcendent*. Since operational science cannot investigate anything immaterial or outside of our universe, it may seem that we are stuck before our investigation even begins. However, we can still use historical science since there is already a Creation Model in place that specifies a transcendent First Cause, and in fact gives us quite a bit of information about this Creator. The worldview based upon the **Judeo-Christian** Bible is the only one to offer textual evidence, first-hand testimony of the Creator, and eye-witness testimony of all subsequent events, so no other creation models will be considered in this series of messages. Since in any historical science investigation all models should be "held loosely", we will not assume biblical authority or inerrancy *a priori*, but reserve the right to do so once the only competing model has been rejected on scientific grounds.

The Evolution Model

By "Evolution Model" we will be referencing what secularists call the *Modern Synthesis*, encompassing *cosmological evolution* (beginning with the Big Bang), *chemical evolution* (the beginning of life), and *biological evolution* (all life forms descending with modification from a common ancestor). According to Prof. Richard Lewontin, "... materialism is absolute, for we cannot allow a Divine Foot in the door". [1] No intelligent cause can be considered. All changes result from random events following laws of physics and chemistry that themselves are self-existent and just happen to be what they are. Molecules self-assemble from atoms that coalesced out of a "quark soup" , formulated over millions of years after the Big Bang's initial energy began to form matter. Molecules increase in complexity, but with no purpose or plan, until they form the amino acids, nucleic acids, lipids and proteins that will over more millions of years eventually lead to living cells able to reproduce themselves. This reproduction is governed only by a process termed "survival of the fittest" which results in a purely natural manner from *natural selection* acting on minor, random genetic changes in each generation.

Implication

Perhaps it has already dawned on you that there are implications depending upon which theoretical model is true. What if our investigation shows that the Creation Model is the best interpretation of the evidence? That implies there is a Creator to Whom we are all accountable.

Message 1 – The Days of Creation

In the beginning God . . .

TEXT: Genesis 1:1-31

Introduction - Comparing the Theoretical Models

Recall in our previous discussion we saw that to scientifically investigate events that happened only in the past, that are not repeatable, and/or are not observable, we must use *historical science* rather than *operational science*. Clearly the question of origins of the universe, mass, energy, time and life can only be investigated using historical science, and logic informs us that there are only three possible models:

a) The universe (heavens and earth) was created;
b) The universe came about by an uncaused event; or
c) The universe is eternal

Astronomical observations and theoretical physics since the early 20th century have essentially ruled out the third possibility (an eternal universe), leaving us with two and only two mutually-exclusive models which we have termed the **Creation Model** and the **Evolution Model**. Since the models contradict each other, the *law of non-contradiction* in logic tells us that if one model is true, the other must be false

Our method will be a straightforward analysis of the claims made by the Creation Model as we move through the first eleven chapters of the book of Genesis. Where a biblical claim differs from the Evolution Model, we will endeavor to ascertain which claim is better supported by the physical evidence we have in the present. Note that both models have the same evidence at their disposal, so the reality is we will be analyzing which model is the best *interpretation* of the evidence. Where one model is supported, the other of necessity is discredited by the same amount.

Gen 1:1 *In the beginning God created the heavens and the earth*

Both models proclaim a beginning to the universe, although secular scientists were brought to this assertion "kicking and screaming" following the undeniable astronomical observations of the 20th century. Both models advocate space, mass, energy and time coming into existence suddenly and simultaneously, but the biblical account seems to imply the universe came *ex nihilo* (from nothing)[92], while the Big Bang portion of the Evolution Model postulates an initial, infinitely "hot dense state" smaller than a proton. Where this putative particle came from is dismissed with some hand-waving by most secular scientists who simply say that such a question is a "singularity" and "outside the realm of science". At least one scientist has theorized that the universe indeed came from "nothing", which he describes as a "quantum fluctuation of a vacuum"[98-99]. The Bible is specific in contending that this First Cause was a pre-existent, all powerful, all-knowing God who must of necessity be outside of the time and space limitations imposed by His creation on His creatures. In this respect, the laws of logic favor the Creation Model. Specifically, the Law of Cause-and-Effect states that every effect that has a beginning must have a cause, and an effect can never be greater than its cause[96-97]. Also, the first and second laws of thermodynamics seem to be violated by a universe that creates itself from nothing and then self-organizes with no agent performing work on it. Score 1 point for Creation.

Gen 1:2 *And the earth was formless and void, and darkness was over the surface of the deep, and the Spirit of God was moving over the surface of the waters.*

The difference in the two models is a bit subtle here. Both envision a planet that is initially "formless" (think "blob"), but the Evolution Model claims dust from exploding stars coagulated like "cosmic dust bunnies"[2], while heating from gravitational tidal forces resulted in a molten, rocky planet that would take millions of years to cool enough to form a solid crust, later to be somehow covered with water (perhaps due to millions of incoming comets). This verse, and other passages in Scripture, imply that the planet was initially water, from which God formed the dry land. The evidence is not conclusive either way. The earth's mantle and outer core are indeed molten rock today, but at the same time seismic research has found there is much water inside the earth (mostly in the form of hydrate compounds). One hallmark of a successful theoretical model is that it is able to make valid predictions. To this end, Dr. Russell Humphries (a creation scientist) used the Creation Model to predict the magnetic field strength of several planets based on the assumption they were initially water with polarized hydrogen atoms. When space probes travelled past these planets, the magnetic fields were measured to be exactly within the error bands predicted by Dr. Humphries, while secular scientists had predicted no magnetic fields at all[165-169]. Score 1 for Creation (OK, maybe only score ½!).

Gen 1:3 – 5 *Then God said, "Let there be light"; and there was light. And God saw that the light was good; and God separated the light from the darkness. And God called the light day, and the darkness He called night. And there was evening and there was morning, one day.*

Any potential harmony between the two models evaporates here. Clearly the Bible is stating the earth existed before there was any light from the sun or stars. Not only that, but the sun and stars will not even exist for three more days! How can either model be supported by evidence that only exists in the present?

In the 1960's, Nobel Prize winner Dr. Arno Penzias (a creationist) and his team discovered what is now called the cosmic microwave background radiation (CMB). This electromagnetic radiation is "light", it's just not within the portion of the spectrum that is visible to the human eye. The Evolution Model postulates that this radiation permeated all of space shortly after the Big Bang, as sub-atomic particles began to form, and thus predates the formation of any stars or galaxies. It turns out that both models predicted this primordial light, but the Creation Model stipulates that it must have been coming from one general direction in order for the rotation of the planet to separate "night" from "day". Biblically the source for this light could only have been God Himself, and indeed multiple passages in Scripture describe God as "light" [e.g., 1John 1:5; Is 2:5; John 1:9]. Since the evidence we have does not unequivocally support either model, we call this one a draw.

Gen 1: 6 – 8 *Then God said, "Let there be an expanse in the midst of the waters, and let it separate the waters from the waters." And God made the expanse, and separated the waters which were below the expanse from the waters which were above the expanse, and it was so. And God called the expanse heaven. And there was evening and there was morning, a second day.*

This enigmatic passage has baffled creationists for thousands of years, mostly due to the uncertain meaning of the Hebrew word *raqiya*, here translated as expanse, but called "firmament" in the King James translation, and which could also be translated as "stretched out thinness". Even the term "heaven" is enigmatic, since Scripture speaks of at least three "heavens". Dr. Henry Morris II, regarded to be the father of modern creation science, equated this expanse with the atmosphere (where birds fly), and theorized the waters above the atmosphere to be a vapor/ice canopy that would have shielded the planet from harmful radiation, stabilized global temperatures, and that ultimately collapsed onto the earth contributing to the Flood of Noah's day. More recently, creation scientists have theorized that the "expanse" is actually all of space, and cite numerous Old Testament passages that describe God "stretching out" the heavens as one would spread and stretch a tent. Secular astronomers acknowledge water ice to be abundant in deep space, and even theorize a region called the Oort Cloud as a source for the short period "dirty snowballs" called comets, but they don't seem to bother themselves as to where that ice came from. The Big Bang theory also postulates a period of cosmic expansion called *inflation* which is needed to rescue the theory from something called the *horizon problem*[155-158]. Since both models specify a period of expansion, as well as waters/ice above and below, and since creationists are not in total agreement on their model, we will score no points for either model here. It is interesting, though, that God spent an entire day of creation in separating the waters and stretching something out. This would seem to imply that more than just Earth's atmosphere is involved here.

Gen 1: 9 – 13

This passage describes the events of the third day where God performs another act of separation, this time gathering the waters below into one place so that dry land could appear. Following this, God causes plants to sprout, already bearing seeds and fruits to ensure their reproduction, and twice calls everything good. Other than the amount of time involved, both models agree on the appearance of continental land mass and ultimate appearance of plants.

However, secular scientists admit that they are at a loss to explain how plants could arise from non-living chemicals in an evolutionary scenario. In one sense, plants are more complicated than animals in that they are *autotrophs*, that is they manufacture their own food from carbon dioxide, water and radiant energy (with 97% efficiency) in order to power their cellular respiration[170-172]. Our most brilliant scientists have been unable to duplicate this process of photosynthesis, let alone explain any plausible pathway by which this could have arisen by itself. Score 1 for Creation.

Gen 1: 14 – 19

In another major departure from the Evolution Model, this account of Day 4 describes God making the sun, moon and stars in the "expanse of the heavens" (giving further credence to the idea that the "expanse" of Day 2 is in fact all of space). The Big Bang cosmology of the Evolution Model asserts that stars (including our sun) formed from primordial hydrogen gas "clumping together" due to the force of gravity until the resulting extreme heat and pressure ignited thermonuclear fusion. The debris left over from the formation and destruction of these stars then provided the material for the rocky planets, moons and other celestial objects. Can historical science tell us which model is correct? Probably not, unless some "smoking gun" could be discovered proving whether stars predated Earth or not. However, we can turn to *operational* science to provide some insight into the question. Calculations based upon the gas laws of physics tell us that gas molecules do not "clump together", but rather the forces of repulsion are tens of thousands of times stronger than the attractive force of gravity[209]. Secular scientists recognize this, of course, and attempt to rescue their model by suggesting that overpressure from a nearby supernova (exploding star) could provide the necessary force for fusion to happen[210]. The problem then is: How did the star that exploded form in the first place? Any theoretical model that requires that the laws of physics be violated cannot be called "scientific", and this model would require billions-times-billions of miracles to happen in order to form the stars we see today. Since both models require miraculous things to happen, it seems that the Creation Model offers the "simplest" miraculous explanation, and according to Occam's Razor should be the preferred model. Score 1 for Creation.

Incidentally, since one of the stated purposes of God's placement of light-givers in the heavens was to provide "light on the earth", the primordial light created in Day 1 was no longer needed for that purpose. Perhaps God's purpose in waiting until Day 4 to make the celestial objects was to demonstrate the futility of all the future pagan false religions that would try to make these objects into deities worthy of worship. Additional stated purposes were to provide for signs (e.g., navigating by the stars); seasons (caused by Earth's orbital motion around the sun coupled with its rotational axis tilt); days (caused by Earth's rotational period producing daylight and darkness every 24 hours); and years (measured from Earth's orbital period, while the moon's orbital period defines the month).

Gen 1: 20 – 23 *Then God said, "Let the waters teem with swarms of living creatures, and let birds fly above the earth in [on the face of] the open expanse of the heavens." And God created the great sea monsters, and every living creature that moves, with which the waters swarmed after their kind, and every winged bird after its kind . . . And there was evening and there was morning, a fifth day.*

Both the Creation and Evolution models agree that living creatures (not including plants) arose in "the waters", but there the similarity ends. The biblical description includes "great sea monsters" which would have included marine mammals like whales, as well as extinct giant marine reptiles like the plesiosaurs. (In fact, the Hebrew word used is *tannin*, which is elsewhere translated as "dragons".) Likewise, the "winged birds" would have included flying mammals like bats, and the extinct flying reptiles like pterosaurs, which according to the Evolution Model would have only evolved much later (as land animals). Creationists would point to the evidence that living creatures only reproduce "after their kind", and that no undisputed *transitional forms* have ever been found in the fossil record that would support all creatures evolving from a common ancestor. Secular scientists claim the geologic column and the vertical order in which fossils are found supports their model of "simple" marine organisms preceding the "more complex" organisms that arose later. For now, we will consider the argument a draw, because as we will see in Message 7, the models fundamentally disagree on the very nature of the fossil record; creationists contending that it merely reflects the order in which organisms were buried, not the order in which they evolved. No points for either model for now.

Gen 1: 24 – 31

On Day 6 God calls for the earth to bring forth all of the land animals, repeating five more times the stipulation that they reproduce "after their kind". Since this would preclude one created "kind" interbreeding with another, the biblical kind must be a higher taxonomic classification than "species", since many hybrids among species have been observed. For example, a zebra can be bred to a horse (producing a "zorse"), but any offspring from such pairings will always be of the horse kind (genus *equus*). Active research is being performed by creation scientists to ascertain the taxonomic limits for the biblical kinds, which for our purposes seem to roughly correspond to the category of families. The goal of this research is to understand how many mating pairs of animals would need to be taken onto the ark to insure survival of the kind through the Flood. Such research is also being done by secular scientists in order to discover pathways that one kind of animal could evolve into another. It is significant that no such pathway has been found in over 150 years of research since Darwin's publication of *On the Origin of Species*. One famous experiment has been bombarding fruit flies with radiation over thousands of generations in order to mutate their genes. While they have produced legless, wingless, two-headed and four-winged fruit flies, they are still fruit flies! No evolutionary change. Score 1 for Creation.

Day 6 also features God forming man (from the earth as we will see in the next message), and creating man in His own image. The Hebrew verb *bara* is used here to indicate man's essence is a new creation, not formed from pre-existing substance. Man is also defined to be male and female, with no "gender neutral" option, and to have dominion over every living creature. Clearly the Creation Model depicts man as unique and superior to every other living organism, while also expected to exercise stewardship over the rest of the creation. Secular scientists have attempted to support their Evolution Model by pointing to "hominid" fossils that they claim are transitional between an ape-like ancestor and *homo sapiens*. But creation scientists, as well as many secular scientists, have shown that these fossils can be dismissed as either extinct apes or modern humans. Moreover, evolutionists have tried in vain to explain within their model the uniquely human characteristics like self-awareness, altruism, aesthetics, and abstract thinking. Score 1 for Creation again!

Conclusion

Admittedly, our score-keeping method is a bit whimsical, so we will abandon it in future messages. The point is that one can analyze and compare the two worldview models in a scientific way, using the usual tools of science: reason and observation guided by experience. If you are here today and have perhaps harbored doubts about the existence of God, I want to encourage you to objectively analyze what has been presented in this message. There is nothing inherently scientific about the Evolution Model. It depends upon miraculous events like a universe creating itself from nothing, and stars self-assembling in violation of known laws of science. On the other hand, envision a Creator who is all-powerful, all-knowing and eternal, who created you as a special person, different from every other human and superior to every other creature on the planet.

Later in this series we will see that He loved you so much that He took on human form to live, suffer and die so that you can be with Him for all eternity. Clearly a God who can speak the entire universe into existence in the very first verse of the Bible is capable of changing your heart to know and to love Him. *Today if you would hear His voice, do not harden your hearts*

Psalm 95: 7-8

Message 2 – Creation of Man

...and man became a living being.

TEXT: Genesis 2: 1 – 25

Introduction

In the previous message we defined two and only two mutually-exclusive theoretical models that can be used to investigate the teachings of Scripture using *historical science*. Evidence that exists only in the present can be examined using the usual tools of science to conclude whether that evidence supports – or fails to support – one model over the other. The evidence examined so far seems to support the Creation Model over the Evolution Model as they relate to the first six days of the universe's history. We will continue analyzing the Creation Model using the Judeo-Christian Bible, contrasting it with the Evolution Model, and weighing the available evidence in light of both models.

The second chapter of Genesis is considered by most biblical scholars to be a recapitulation of the prologue of Chapter 1, with an expansion on the culminating product of the prologue: *mankind*.

Gen 2: 1 – 3

The first three verses summarize God's work of the first six days, and describe His resting on the seventh day from all creative acts; blessing and sanctifying the seventh day. The original Hebrew text uses the verb *bara* to indicate fiat creation from no preceding materials, and the verb *asah* to indicate something "made" from pre-existing substances. Thus verse 3 uses both verbs in summarizing God's work of the first six days. The inference here is that God is finished "creating", although He will continue to "make" or to "form" (Hebrew verb *yatsar*). While secular scientists would not agree with the biblical account of events, they nonetheless are in universal agreement that nothing "new" is coming into existence anywhere in the universe, and have codified this into a scientific law: The First Law of Thermodynamics, which states that matter and energy may change forms, but the total amount in the universe remains constant, without being either created or destroyed. Ironically, the Evolution Model must violate this fundamental law of physics in order to initiate the Big Bang from nothing, thus requiring secular scientists to violate their own scientific laws in order to even get their theoretical model off the ground!

These verses also explain the origin of our seven-day week. While the idea of a Sabbath day of rest will not surface again until the time of Moses (in the second book of the Bible), there is no other logical explanation for a seven-day week. Every other unit of measuring time is based upon periodic astronomical events or integer divisions of these events (year, month, day, hour, minute, second). There is nothing that would suggest a seven-day week in any astronomical or terrestrial periodic phenomenon. Thus, our desk calendars provide us with a silent testimony of evidence supporting these verses of the Bible.

Gen 2: 4 *This is the account of the heavens and the earth when they were created, in the day that the Lord God made earth and heaven.*

In our first message we defined the Creation Model of the Judeo-Christian Bible as being the only model to offer textual evidence, first-hand testimony of the Creator, and eye-witness testimony of all subsequent events. Here for the first time, we see a pattern that will repeat itself multiple times throughout the book of Genesis where the identity of the one giving testimony is given. Scholars consider passages such as this to be *internal evidence*, within the Scriptures themselves, that what is being presented is historical narrative and not metaphorical or mythological. According to the *tablet theory*, in authoring Genesis, Moses was probably the *editor* of far older documents. Eleven times we see his editorial statement, "This is the account of . . . ", or perhaps a better translation is in the King James version, "These are the generations of . . . ". These *toledot* statements, as they are called, identify the divisions between the different source documents Moses used[17]. There is substantial disagreement among biblical scholars as to whether the *toledot* statement marks the beginning or the end of an historical narrative. This first of the *toledot* statements is the only one that does not name a human author (such as the second one does in Gen 5:1, "This is the book of the generations of Adam"). Since only God himself would have first-hand knowledge of the events described in Genesis 1, this first *toledot* would indicate that God must be the author, either dictating the text for Adam to record, or perhaps writing it on tablets with His own finger as He did with the Ten Commandments on Mount Sinai. While this does not constitute *scientific* evidence in the strict sense, nonetheless historians always give great weight to strong internal evidence when analyzing ancient texts to determine if they are truly historical narratives[47ff].

Gen 2: 5 – 6

While plants were created on Day 3, these verses are describing what the earth was like before man in terms of what was *not* there. While there were grasses, herbs and fruit trees, there were no "shrubs" or "plants" of the *field*, in other words, no field crops that would have required man to cultivate them[296]. There was no precipitation in the form of rain, but there was a mist that would rise from the earth and water the ground, evidently from some subterranean source. There is no significant disagreement, other than timeframes, between the Creation and Evolution Models here, since secularists would agree that crop cultivation was an invention of mankind after the appearance of other types of plants. For example, the New World corn that natives introduced to the first European settlers was cultivated from plants that have no resemblance to what we call corn today.

Gen 2: 7 *Then the Lord God formed man of the dust from the ground, and breathed into his nostrils the breath of life, and man became a living being [soul].*

It is almost as though God is throwing a bone to the evolutionists here. Man is "formed" (from the Hebrew verb *yatsar*) from the same earth elements as other vertebrates and primates, and in fact man shares many of the fundamental building blocks of cells with these other life forms: nucleic acids, amino acids, lipids, proteins, enzymes, etc. Other animals also possess the "breath" (Hebrew *neshama*) and "soul"(Hebrew *nephesh*).

But man's breath (same word as "spirit") and soul were imparted to him by God *directly*, rather than indirectly as imparted to the animals. If man's body had been derived from an animal's body by any kind of evolutionary process, he would have already possessed the *nephesh*, rather than "becoming a living soul" when God gave him the breath of life[301ff]. The Creation Model refutes the Evolution Model here, but what evidence is there of this human exceptionalism? We have already mentioned that being made "in the image of God" results in human traits that evolutionists are at a total loss to explain. It is the *mind*, not the brain, that distinguishes man from other primates. While quite similar in a material, anatomical sense, the ape brain is incapable of complex language, mathematics, religion, philosophy, logic, literature, art, music, history, science, engineering, or countless other abstract abilities. The very fact that you are able to comprehend this message at all is evidence that Genesis 2:7 is a complete refutation of the Evolution Model.

Gen 2: 8 – 14

These verses begin with describing God planting a garden in Eden, which was apparently "east" of where Adam currently was. God placed the man in the garden and specially planted it with trees remarkable for their beauty as well as for being "good for food". Since God had already planted vegetation that was edible for man and animals (Gen 1: 29-30), the plantings in the Garden must have been especially desirable for mankind (who alone had the capacity to appreciate beauty). Two trees in particular are mentioned that were designed particularly for man: the tree of life, which apparently would extend the human lifespan indefinitely, and the tree of "the knowledge of good and evil". Since animals have no moral compass allowing them to differentiate between that which is good versus that which is evil, this tree would only impact man – and then only if evil actually existed – which it could not at this time since God had just pronounced everything He created as "very good". Apparently, Eden was at some elevation higher than the surrounding land since a river flowed from it, dividing into four rivers that watered the rest of the land. (While two of these rivers had names we recognize today, they cannot be the same rivers since the Flood to come will totally change the topography of the earth.)[316ff]

There is no parallel in the Evolution Model with the information in this passage, so we must ask, "Is there evidence today that supports the idea of indefinite human longevity being physiologically feasible?", and furthermore, "Is there evidence today that supports the notion that mankind's unique "moral compass" could have arisen from an ape-like intellect as required by the Evolution Model?"

Recent genetic research on aging has shed considerable light on ways in which it can be slowed, and at least theoretically stopped[467ff]. As our bodies' cells reproduce themselves over and over, degradation to the cellular genome gradually accumulates due to "copying errors", much like photocopies of photocopies get progressively more corrupted. Such cellular degradation is typically what we call "aging". Research in molecular genetics shows that chromosomes are "protected" by long strings of repetitive sequences at their ends called *telomeres.* It is found that as we age, our telomeres get shorter, leading to a number of nutrition supplements now being advertised as having the ability to fight aging by energizing the telomerase machinery that repairs the telomeres. Whether these products actually perform as advertised is debatable, but the fact that they are developed from natural herbs does lend credence to the claim of the Creation Model that a tree once had fruit containing such nutrients.

As mentioned earlier, secular scientists have been unsuccessful in explaining how uniquely human traits encompassing immaterial concepts like morality or beauty evolved with only mutation and natural selection driving their evolution. The Bible explains that the material aspect of man which God "formed", arose simultaneously with the "spirit" or "soul" of man (*nephesh*) which God breathed into him. While evolutionists would certainly not be satisfied with such a supernatural origin for the "knowledge of good and evil", it is significant that the Creation Model explains it explicitly and right up front, while the Evolution Model offers no explanation other that some lame "just so" stories.

Gen 2: 15 – 17 *Then the Lord God took the man and put him in the Garden of Eden to cultivate and keep it. And the Lord God commanded the man, saying, "From any tree of the garden you may eat freely; but from the tree of the knowledge of good and evil you shall not eat, for in the day that you eat from it you shall surely die."*

"Good and evil" is a *merism*, two opposites standing for the whole range in between; for example, "Heavens and earth" (Gen 1:1) or "good or bad" (Gen 31:24). This merism also carries the concept of having the power to decide for oneself what is, or is not, in one's best interests, and in that respect, to be like God. Animals have no capacity to distinguish good from evil, or to make moral decisions about what may or may not be in their best interests. Their behavior is programmed into their brains. Note that only by disobeying God's command could mankind know evil, which up to this time did not exist in the material world since God had declared everything that He made to be very good. A "knowledge of good and evil" would necessarily follow from eating the forbidden fruit, since evil is fundamentally merely rejection of God's Word. Disobedience would itself constitute an experimental knowledge of evil.

While we might conjecture that there was something nutritionally unique about the fruit on the tree of life, we need make no such conjecture about this forbidden fruit. No matter what it was, eating of it was an act of disobedience, which would define evil and ultimately result in death. The meaning of "in the day you eat of it you shall surely die" has been debated for centuries, since Adam lived for another 930 years after he ate. One explanation that seems consistent with operational science is that God, at that moment, would remove some of His sustaining power that would have otherwise prevented the corruption and mutations that would degrade the human genome in Adam's generation, and every generation to follow. In this interpretation, dying began at the moment of disobedience, and continues to this day in the manifestations of so many diseases and abnormalities caused by errors in our genetic coding. Presently our genes accumulate about 30 to 100 mutations per generation, most of them not harmful. But at that rate of what Dr. John Sanford has termed *genetic entropy*, the human species should go extinct in less than 10,000 years[686]. The fact that we are still here baffles most secular scientists, but is consistent with the Creation Model of less than 10,000 years of human habitation on Earth.

Gen 2: 18 – 20

In these verses God demonstrates something to Adam that is "not good" in His very good creation: that he has no suitable mate comparable to what the animals had. It was "not good" in the sense of *incompleteness*, not in the sense of evil. To bring the point home, God brings every kind of animal that could conceivably be a suitable companion for Adam to name. He names them, but obviously none would be a suitable mate.

Skeptics scoff at the idea of Adam naming all the animals, but the Bible only mentions him naming "field animals", "cattle" and birds. If the goal was for Adam to find a suitable mate, then clearly there would be no need to bring arthropods (90% of all species), reptiles, amphibians or fish. As we'll see when we discuss the animals on Noah's ark, the ancestors of today's "kinds" of animals would be quite a manageable number to name. For example, genetic science has shown that all 37 species in the modern cat family likely descended from an ancestral "Adam and Eve" of the cat kind[3]. One might indeed wonder, "Why bring the 'birds of the air'?". But man has a long history of domesticating birds for agriculture (chickens, quail, turkeys), for hunting (falconers), and even for companionship (think Robinson Crusoe's parrot or Grandma's parakeet).

Secular scientists today spend an inordinate amount of time in classifying creatures that they find, since finding a new species and being able to name it for the first time is a feather in any biologist's cap. The competition for this is so fierce that it is not uncommon to find the same species has been given several different names.

It is consistent with science that the first human would be involved in naming other creatures in carrying out his dominion mandate.

Gen 2: 21 – 25 *So the Lord God caused a deep sleep to fall upon the man, and he slept; then He took one of his ribs, and closed up the flesh at that place. And the Lord God fashioned into a woman the rib which He had taken from the man, and brought her to the man. And the man said, "This is now bone of my bones,*
And flesh of my flesh;
She shall be called Woman,
Because she was taken out of Man."
For this cause a man shall leave his father and his mother, and shall cleave to his wife; and they shall become one flesh. And the man and his wife were both naked and were not ashamed.

This account of the world's first surgery inspired the Scottish doctor Sir James Young Simpson to found the science of anesthesiology, discovering that chloroform would put people to sleep and remove the pain sensation [328]. Thus, to argue that the Creation Model is a "science stopper" denies the fact that the Creation Model actually provides the basis for operational science, since it advocates an orderly creation that man is capable of mastering; in fact, the dominion mandate *requires* man to engage in science.

The manner in which God "fashioned" woman (Hebrew *banah*) has both theological and scientific implications [329].

Theologically, woman is not of inferior substance, but is of his bone and flesh, reinforcing Gen 1: 27 's statement that both man and woman were created in God's image. At the same time this account reinforces the biblical teaching that Adam is the Federal Head of the whole human race: every other human who has ever lived is a descendant of Adam (including Eve).

Scientifically, it is likely that God used Adam's genetic information to "fashion" (or "build") Eve. Clearly, He would have had to replace Adam's Y chromosome with a second X chromosome to generate the female XX configuration. This does not imply that , other than the sex chromosome, Eve would be a clone of Adam. It is likely that God created both Adam and Eve with paired chromosomes, just as all people have today, meaning that at every position ("locus") on any chromosome they could each have a different type (or "allele") of the gene, producing a staggering number of genetic combinations that could result from the first human couple [330]. Current genetic research has revealed that the mitochondrion (an organelle in human cells) possesses its own DNA, and is inherited only through the mother's line. By invoking the idea of a "genetic clock" reflecting accumulated mutations, scientists have found that all mitochondrial DNA in humans today is likely descended from a single "mitochondrial Eve" (their term) [385]. Similarly, analysis of the Y chromosome, passed only through the father's line, indicates a single "Y chromosome Adam" (again their term) in our past [386]. Secular scientist hurriedly add that these ancient humans were not contemporaneous, and merely represent the only lineages of *homo sapiens* that did not die out.

However, this is special pleading that is not supported by any evidence, meaning that strong scientific evidence exists for the Creation Model. Moreover, the Evolution Model is incapable of even explaining the evolutionary origin for sexual reproduction, let alone any pathway by which the human genome could ever become fixed in a putative population of apes. The number of genetic changes that would need to occur to get from an ape to a human number in the hundreds of millions [386], but genetic changes in one generation are often observed to disappear in subsequent generations, with the general rule being "variation about a mean" rather than "upward and continuous genetic changes providing survival benefit" as required by the Evolution Model.

Further evidence supporting this biblical account concerns the human rib. The rib is the one bone in the human body that will readily grow back! That is , provided the covering membrane called the *periosteum* is left intact. Thoracic surgeons routinely remove a rib to operate on organs inside the chest. Surgeons performing bone grafts typically remove a rib for the bone material. When subsequent bone grafts are needed, they will return to the same place (to minimize scarring) and remove *the same rib*, which had grown back [331].

Also, the mention of "his wife" indicates that the union between Adam and Eve was the first example of marriage, a sacrament ordained and blessed by God Himself. The husband was to "leave" (or "forsake") his parents and "cleave" (literally "stick like glue") to his wife. That the two "shall become one flesh" shows that sexual intercourse was ordained by God before the Fall, but only in the context of those who are held in the "glue" of marriage. Jesus later confirmed and elaborated on marriage intended to be between one man and one woman for life (Matt 19:3-9 and Mark 10: 2-9), and that any other arrangement devised by man would be equivalent to adultery. One hardly needs to be a scientist to see the wisdom of the original plan. Any casual observer looking at today's statistics indicating over half of all marriages are in tatters would have to admit God's original plan was superior to any other.

Finally, the innocence portrayed by the first couple being unashamed of their nakedness is only seen today in the very young (toddlers) or adults suffering from some form of dementia. For the rest of us, we have an innate desire to cover our nakedness, the same urge that we will see in Adam and Eve following their knowledge of their sin.

Conclusion

The previous message provided evidence supporting the concept of a Creator (Creation Model) as opposed to the notion of self-assembly from nothing (Evolution Model). In this message we have seen evidence supporting the concept of man being specially created "in the image of God" according to the biblical account of the Creation Model, as opposed to man having evolved from an ancestor shared with other primates.

If you are a product of the public education system, or even most private schools and colleges, you have been indoctrinated into the Evolution Model for as long as you can remember. Whether you now consider yourself an atheist, an agnostic, or some version of theist, as an honest person you must admit to having had serious doubts about the wild claims of those advocating the Evolution Model. The apostle Paul told the Roman pagans that they were "without excuse" in denying God's "eternal power and divine nature" because these could be "clearly seen, being understood through what has been made", [Rom 2:20]. With all the scientific evidence at our disposal today, we have even less "excuse" than the pagans of Paul's time.

Your human brain is the most highly ordered arrangement of matter in the universe, with more electrical connections than the worldwide web. But more important than the physical matter of your brain is the God-given *mind* somehow embedded within it. It is with this mind that God desires you to know Him and to have fellowship with Him, something that no animal is empowered to do. Like Adam and Eve, you have the ability to choose to follow God or to rebel against Him. Because you have freedom of will, unlike the animals whose brains are pre-programmed, you must make that decision. No one, not even God, can make that choice for you. Why not make that decision right now? "You do not know what your life will be like tomorrow" [Ja 4:14], "for tomorrow we may die" [Is 22:13].

Message 3 – The Fall of Man

And to dust you shall return

TEXT: Genesis 3: 1 – 24

Introduction

Here begins the most tragic chapter of the Bible. In it is the preamble for all the death, disease and suffering to come in the once-perfect creation. Most secular scientists, even those who subscribe to some form of theism, scoff at the concept of a talking serpent, or even the concept of Satan himself. It was mentioned in the first message that spiritual phenomena are outside the scope of scientific investigation, but we can still use the ordinary tools of science to see if the evidence we find in the world today is *consistent* with the Creation Model and/or the Evolution Model. For the most part, we will see in this message that either model can offer an explanation for the evidence, and that's OK. Quite often in science we encounter evidence that is inconclusive. That does not necessarily support one model over the other, but if the evidence does not tend to falsify a model, then the model is considered still viable.

Gen 3: 1 *Now the serpent was more crafty than any beast of the field that the Lord God had made. And he said to the woman, "Indeed, has God said, 'You shall not eat any [every] tree of the garden'?"*

The implication here is the serpent co-opted by Satan was originally a "beast" which will later become a "creeping thing" after losing its legs. This would of course have involved some genetic changes in the serpent's DNA. Genetic research today is revealing more and more instances of genes being switched off or on by the inclusion or deletion of genetic markers called *methylation groups*, and indeed there are reports in the literature of snakes being born with legs (non-functional, of course), and lizards that have snake-like bodies, which would be consistent with the Creation Model[4].

More troublesome is the idea of the serpent and Eve being able to communicate with a complete language syntax. A famous gorilla named Koko was said to have mastered 1,000 signs of American sign language, but entirely lacked any understanding of syntax (word order, tense, recursion, etc.). In a few more verses God will put "enmity" between the serpent (and Satan) and "the woman", and following the Flood, He will put the fear of man into the rest of the animals. This would explain the lack of communicable language between man and the other animals today, and is consistent with either model. A much greater problem exists for the Evolution Model in explaining how language ability ever evolved in the first place, and why it apparently only arose in humans. Of course, there is some evidence of animal communication in creatures like dolphins, and researchers are attempting to decipher their language code, which actually might be quite complex. However, even if true, this does not particularly support one model over another.

The methodology Satan used to deceive Eve is classic, and one still in wide use today. He begins by questioning God's character while utterly misquoting Him. An analogy today would be the skeptic who asks, "Would a loving God allow all the suffering we see in our world today?". More on Satan's methods momentarily.

Gen 3: 2 – 3

To her credit, Eve immediately corrects Satan's misquote, but then inserts one of her own, saying that God said they must not eat of it *or touch it*, lest they die. While we are instructed not to add to or subtract from God's Word [Rev 22: 18-19], most scholars are willing to cut Eve some slack here. God gave the original instruction to Adam before Eve was even created. In relaying the command, Adam may have added, "Don't even touch it!" to emphasize the importance of the prohibition, much as we might tell a child, "Don't touch those cupcakes," when all we really mean is, "Don't eat any of those cupcakes."

Gen 3: 4 – 5 *And the serpent said to the woman, "You surely shall not die! For God knows that in the day that you eat from it your eyes will be opened, and you will be like God, knowing good and evil."*

Satan moves from misleading questions to an outright lie – the first lie recorded in Scripture, but wraps it in a partial truth that they would "be like God, knowing good and evil". Again, we see a classic methodology in use, that is still widely used today in the form of "fake news". Ardent evolutionists today follow the same methodology: First, raise doubts about the wisdom, character, and even existence of God; second make statements (like the Evolution Model) that directly contradict the Word of God; and third, advance the idea that disregarding God's Word (Creation Model) will result in a greater good (belief in the more enlightened religion of materialism). The fact that today's methodology is the same one that Satan has used throughout the ages is self-evident, and both theoretical models support it, although in different ways.

Gen 3: 6 *And when the woman saw that the tree was good for food, and that it was pleasing to the eyes, and a tree to be desired to make one wise, she took of the fruit thereof, and did eat, and gave also unto her husband with her, and he did eat.*

The temptation was three-fold, appealing to the body ("good for food"), the soul ("pleasing to the eyes"), and the spirit ("make one wise"). The same formula was used by Satan to test Jesus in the wilderness (Luke 4: 1-12) and was warned about by the apostle in 1John 2:16 ("the lust of the flesh and the lust of the eyes and the boastful pride of life"). The fact that three passages of Scripture, by three different authors separated by thousands of years, acknowledge the same lethal formula for tempting mankind is strong evidential support for divine inspiration, supporting the Creation Model over any competing model devised by man. It has been argued that Eve was the first to compromise God's Word with fallible science, in that she made her own interpretation of sense data authoritative over His Word. As such, she could be considered the patron saint of the Evolution Model!

A key point that differentiates the Judeo-Christian Creation Model from any other religion is the concept of *original sin*. The apostle Paul speaks at length about this in his letter to the church at Rome. Even though Eve's sin precedes Adam's, it is from the sin of this one man that we acquire our *sin nature*. Prior to this sin, Adam and Eve had the *power of contrary choice*, in other words they had the ability not to sin. As a result of this sin humanity lost the power of contrary choice, which meant that they could not perfectly (consistently and completely) go against their sin nature. People today do not get their sin nature by sinning; they sin because of their sin nature[356]. This will not change until the redeemed in Christ acquire their Eternal State and no longer have an ability to sin.

Skeptics who seek to discredit the Creation Model by lumping Christianity with all the other (false) religions are committing the logical fallacy of *equivocation.* The Christian religion is unlike any other, since all the other world religions teach that man's nature is basically good, and that through performing the proper works a person can achieve their heavenly reward. The Christian concept of original sin recognizes that man in his sin nature is helpless and worthy only of death without the salvation offered through Jesus Christ. Check out today's news to see if the evidence supports man's "basically good" nature or man's sin nature!

Gen 3: 7 – 13

This passage begins with the first humans realizing that they were naked, and in contrast to Gen 2:25, they are ashamed and fashion loincloths or girdles from fig leaves. In what was apparently a daily custom, they hear God walking in the garden in the "cool" (or "breeze") of the day, and hide. God asks them a series of question which clearly are not designed to inform Him (since He is omniscient), but more likely designed to elicit confession and repentance of their sin. Instead, they play the blame game, he blaming her and she blaming the serpent.

Gen 3: 14 – 15 *And the Lord God said to the serpent, "Because you have done this, cursed are you more than all cattle, and more than every beast of the field; on your belly shall you go and dust shall you eat all the days of your life; and I will put enmity between you and the woman, and between your seed and her seed; he shall bruise [crush] you on the head, and you shall bruise him on the heel.*

God's first pronouncement of judgment is on the serpent whose body Satan had co-opted. Apparently once a "shining" specimen among the animals, it would now be the most loathsome of all and would crawl in and eat the dust of the ground. It is interesting to note that in spite of having no arms or legs, snakes are nonetheless superbly adapted to survive in their environment to this day, an indication that God still cares even for the creatures we consider loathsome. Also, snakes actually do eat dust[362]. Scientists have discovered that the flicking tongue transfers non-volatile chemicals in the environment (that could not otherwise be detected by smell) to make physical contact with the Jacobson's organ, a matching pair of sensors inside the mouth. While the Evolution Model would attempt to offer an explanation for this, the Creation Model actually *predicts* it.

After cursing the serpent, God now deals with the real culprit, Satan. Scripture passages like Ez 28; Heb 1; Rev 12 and others inform us that Satan was originally created as the highest of the angels, the anointed cherub covering the very throne of God in heaven. He, as well as the other angels were created to be ministering spirits to humanity. Not content with this subservient role, Satan led a third of the angels to rebel against God, seeking to become God himself. God therefore "cast him to the ground", allowing him to tempt the very ones he had been created to serve.

The reference to the "seed" of a woman is considered by biblical scholars to be the first *messianic prophecy*. The biblical norm is to trace genealogies through the *fathers'* line, so this reference to the seed of a woman is unique in Scripture. The prophecy was fulfilled thousands of years later by the virgin birth of the promised Messiah, without a human father. The nail driven through Christ's heel, and His subsequent vanquishing of Satan's power by His resurrection (with total victory still awaiting the final Consummation) are evidences of additional fulfillment. While the Evolution Model denies the historicity of any of this, fulfilled prophecies are nonetheless successful predictions of the Creation Model. Since the promised Seed would not inherit the sin nature of Adam, this is the only *scientific* way that a suitable sinless sacrifice could be made for man's sins, and thus constitutes scientific evidence in support of the Creation Model.

Gen 3: 16 *To the woman He said, "I will greatly multiply your pain in childbirth, in pain you shall bring forth children; yet your desire shall be for your husband, and he shall rule over you.*

God's judgment on the woman relates to childbirth and her marital relationship. Presumably childbirth would not have been as painful were it not for the Fall. Some pain is not necessarily a bad thing; body builders, for example, typically consider some residual pain to be the sign of a good workout. Childbirth stimulates endorphins that reduce pain and produce a sense of well-being[369]. But clearly God must have introduced a change to Eve's body, and presumably also in her DNA so it would be passed on to her descendants. Dr. David Menton, after describing in his DVD lecture what has been happening in the nine months of fetal development, then compares the final moments before birth to the guy who built a boat in his garage and then realized it would not be able to fit going out through the door![5] God's "fix" to this problem was designing a mechanism by which the mother's cervix could dilate to allow the baby to pass. Atheist evolutionist Richard Dawkins points to this as an example of poor design, in effect ridiculing the notion that humans are designed to begin with. However, in the context of the Creation Model, it is actually supporting evidence.

Gen 3: 17 – 19 *Then to Adam He said, " . . . Cursed is the ground because of you; in toil you shall eat of it all the days of your life. Both thorns and thistles it shall grow for you; and you shall eat the plants of the field; by the sweat of your face you shall eat bread, till you return to the ground, because from it you were taken; for you are dust, and to dust you shall return.*

God's first judgment on Adam is to curse the ground. Adam had dominion over all creation, so when Adam fell, the whole creation suffered; "groaning" as Paul put it in Romans 8. "Thorns and thistles" clearly did not exist before Adam sinned, and studies today reveal that a thorn is actually a modified leaf, tightly curled upon itself, indicative of a post-Fall disruption of the growth mechanism for some leaves[374ff]. While this alone is evidence in support of the Creation Model, there is even more evidence for design in the fact that *flatness* of leaves is even more difficult to explain from an evolutionary point of view. Flatness requires that a leaf's growth be carefully coordinated between the leaf's central regions and its edges. Recent discoveries show that balancing these two growth rates is regulated by genes, and that it is remarkable to balance them so precisely, since there are so many other ways by which they could be unbalanced.

The second part of the curse on Adam is that he would no longer be able to simply "cultivate and keep" a succulent, God-planted garden, but would have to toil mightily to raise field crops like barley and rye from which to make bread (fighting thorns and thistles all the while). Much of the world might have faced starvation in the early 1960's had it not been for the Green Revolution that greatly increased crop yields through improved farming practices, fertilizers, pesticides, herbicides, and new plant varieties. These extraordinary measures, that farmers still must follow, comprise modern evidence in support of the curse of the Creation Model, while in the Evolution Model these improvements should have evolved all by themselves.

The third part of Adam's curse spells out exactly how the consequence of "death" would manifest itself. The largest portion of biomass on the planet today consists of the "decomposers" (scavengers, termites, other insects and arthropods, micro-organisms of all types, soil bacteria, etc.), constantly converting organic matter into its constituent compounds ("dust"). The same basic nutrients that adult organisms consume and ultimately convert into their offspring are the ones constantly returned to the ground by way of decomposition and death. What more evidence for "dust to dust" could we ask for?

Gen 3: 20 – 21 *Now the man called his wife's name Eve* [life]*, because she was the mother of all the living. And the Lord God made garments of skin for Adam and his wife and clothed them.*

In the previous message we looked at the evidence for there being a "mother of all the living" in the study of mitochondrial DNA that leads scientists to postulate a "mitochondrial Eve" as the maternal ancestor of everyone alive today. In the Evolution Model it must be an incredible stroke of luck that one maternal line, and only one, would survive over nearly a million years of human evolution. The Creation Model, on the other hand, *requires* it.

We saw at the beginning of this chapter that shame over their sin caused Adam and Eve to want to cover their nakedness with fig leaves. That God provided them with garments made from the skin (hide, pelt, etc.) of animals indicates that He must have killed animals. It is possible that he killed them in front of Adam and Eve so they would understand the horror and meaning of death. Physically He clothed their nakedness, but spiritually He also covered their sin by making for them the first blood atonement. Hebrews 9:22 says that "without the shedding of blood there is no forgiveness", and we see this theme continually in Scripture from Cain and Abel right up to the shed blood of Jesus Christ Himself. Clothing must be important to God, since we will be wearing clothes even in heaven according to the Book of Revelation. Both Paul and Peter cautioned Christian women to dress modestly in order to not fan the flames of lust in men. Nearly every culture on Earth today practices some clothing convention, and associates blatant nudity with lawlessness. While the Evolution Model does not make any particular statement about this practice (other than clothing providing a survival benefit), the Creation Model is entirely consistent with it.

Gen 3: 22 – 24

The closing verses of this chapter describe God driving Adam and Eve from the garden in order that they not "take also from the tree of life, and eat, and live forever". Furthermore, He stationed cherubim and a flaming sword to guard the entrance to the garden. Cherubim are the highest of the angels, and usually are associated with the presence of God Himself. Some scholars associate the flaming sword with God's Shekinah Glory, later to be manifest in the burning bush and pillar of fire in the Book of the Exodus. For this reason, it is hypothesized that man would continue to return to this spot to worship and offer sacrifices for atonement for generations to come. The fact that the rivers flowed out of Eden indicates it must have been on high ground, which would explain why only one entrance would have to be guarded, assuming it was only accessible from one direction.

Of course, the Flood resulted in there being no evidence of Eden at all in the present world. No one claims that the names of two of the rivers still being in use today constitutes evidence for the original rivers, but it is possible that Noah and his descendants remembered those names and used them to memorialize the world they once knew. This argument is philosophical, though, and not scientific. Another philosophical point worth noting is that death was actually a blessing to prevent man from living forever alienated from God. For this reason, we should be thankful that there is no remnant of the tree of life today (despite the claims of some manufacturers of nutritional supplements). However, we shall admit that no evidence in our world today supports these last few verses in the Creation Model.

Conclusion

This most tragic book of the Bible shows us how, in the words of the apostle Paul, "*through one man sin entered into the world, and death through sin, and so death spread to all men, because all sinned . . .*" [Rom 5:12]. But God in His love, grace and mercy also gives us hope in this book. We will not live apart from Him forever in our sin. The promised Seed of a woman is the One through whose obedience we will be made righteous to eternal life [Rom 5: 19-21]. *God demonstrates His own love toward us, in that while we were yet sinners, Christ died for us. Much more then, having now been justified by His blood, we shall be saved from the wrath of God through Him."* [Rom 5: 8-9].

Do you know for certain that if you die tonight as a sinner, you can still live eternally with Him? You can know that – right now – if you are willing to take one step of faith. Scripture assures us very clearly, "*that if you confess with your mouth Jesus as Lord, and believe in your heart that God raised Him from the dead, you shall be saved.*" [Rom 10:9]

Is there any reason you cannot take that step of faith right now?

Message 4 – Conflict and People Increase

. . . sin is crouching at the door

TEXT: Genesis 4: 1 – 5: 1A

Introduction

So far in this series we have examined the Creation Model and the Evolution Model as two competing *theoretical models* and their respective claims regarding origin of the universe, origin of life, origin of *Homo sapiens* and the origin of mankind's sin nature (not specifically addressed in the Evolution Model).

Scripture (Creation Model) does not tell us explicitly how much time has elapsed between the Creation Week and the Fall, but we can infer some things from what has been written[345ff]. Clearly Cain inherits his father's sin nature, so he must have been conceived after the Fall. At the same time there is no indication that Adam and Eve would have disobeyed God's command to "Be fruitful and multiply" in Gen 1:28, implying that very few (if any) of Eve's fertility cycles would have gone by before the first conception of human life. However, enough time must have elapsed so that it would have been a custom of God to walk in the garden with the first humans. It is generally agreed among scholars that not more than a few weeks would have elapsed between God's declaring his creation "very good" and the Fall, and that Cain would have been conceived in that timeframe. And now begins a further unfolding of the tragedy begun by Adam's sin.

Gen 4: 1 – 2a *Now the man [Adam] had relations with his wife Eve, and she conceived and gave birth to Cain, and she said, "I have gotten a manchild [man] with [the help of the Lord." And again she gave birth to his brother Abel.*

Bible translators have struggled with this passage. There is clearly a play on words in her naming of Cain, since the Hebrew word for "have gotten" or "acquire" is very similar. The literal translation of Eve's statement is, "I have gotten a man: YHWH", or "I have received a man, namely Jehovah". Many scholars have suggested that Eve mistakenly took God's first messianic prophesy - for a Redeemer to come through "the seed of the woman" - to be fulfilled with the birth of her first son. While her theology was accurate, her timing and application were not, since the promised birth would not occur for another 4,000 years. Martin Luther held that, "her words show that she was a pious woman who believed the promise of the coming . . . Savior. Therefore, she did not call him a son, but the Man, the Lord, whom God promised and gave [to her]."[406ff]

It probably did not take Eve long to realize that Cain was not the promised Messiah, and this is suggested by the naming of her next-named son – and probably the second-born. The Hebrew word corresponding to "Abel" means "vanity" , and this would be explained by Eve's disillusionment that she was not to be the mother of the Messiah.

Other than the details laid out in Scripture, the evolutionist would not disagree that - however the first humans arose - they would have to very soon bear offspring or the species would immediately go extinct. In that sense, there is no inherent conflict in the major tenets of the two theoretical models so far.

Gen 4: 2B – 5A *And Abel was a keeper of flocks, but Cain was a tiller of the ground. So it came about in the course of time [at the end of days] that Cain brought an offering to the Lord of the fruit of the ground. And Abel, on his part, also brought of the firstlings of his flock and of their fat portions. And the Lord had regard for Abel and for his offering; but for Cain and for his offering He had no regard.*

Clearly some considerable time has elapsed between verses 2A and 2B, since both Cain and Abel are adults, well established in their professions. In the next chapter we will learn that the next-named son, Seth, was born when Adam and Eve were 130 years old and according to Eve, was a replacement for the murdered Abel, so the logical inference is that well over a century has passed. The phrase translated, "in the course of time" literally means, "at the end of days", implying that sacrifices were being offered at regularly appointed times[410ff]. Adam and Eve would surely have instructed their children on what sort of blood offerings God would expect to atone for sins, based upon His model of supplying them with animal skins to cover their nakedness. As the elders of the first generation, Cain and Abel must have been making appropriate offerings for some time, very likely at the very gate to Eden where God's Shekinah Glory gave a visual manifestation of His presence. The fact that this is the first time in decades that God had no regard for Cain's offering indicates that he had departed from making suitable blood offerings, apparently thinking he could substitute "fruit of the ground" instead.

Anthropologically, we see evidence on every continent except Antarctica that humankind took very seriously God's preference for blood sacrifice, although as false religions spread and multiplied, this became distorted into the practicing of human – and even child – sacrifice. While this is consistent with the Creation Model, it is not necessarily evidence in support of it, since the Evolution Model would point to any kind of sacrifice to any kind of "god" as indicative of "ignorance and superstition" that we just need to evolve our way out of.

Biologically, there is an interesting side note in this passage[410]. The animals that Abel kept were the Hebrew kind *tso'n*, which includes both sheep and goats. While these are distinct species today, they were apparently originally of the same Hebrew kind (*min*), since even today they can interbreed and produce a hybrid "geep", and God had ordained that animals could only reproduce "after their kind". Note that these animals would not have been kept for meat at this time, since mankind was still instructed to be vegetarian (Gen 1:29). They could have been raised to supply milk, wool, or hides for clothes and insulation. Later on, as the two species were bred to specialize for different purposes, it became necessary for shepherds to keep them separate, a practice Jesus referred to metaphorically in Matt 25:32. Again this is only evidence for consistency, but it is strong evidence inasmuch as it shows *internal* consistency within Scripture between Genesis and the gospels, as well as *external* consistency with what has been learned through genetics and animal breeding.

Gen 4: 5B – 7 *So Cain became very angry and his countenance fell. Then the Lord said to Cain, "Why are you angry? And why has your countenance fallen? If you do well, will not your* *countenance be lifted up? And if you do not do well, sin is crouching at the door; and its desire is for you, but you must master it."*

As before in the Garden, God's questions are designed not to inform Him, but to offer Cain a way to "redeem" himself. The implication is that if Cain can get over his anger and "do well" by offering a proper sacrifice, he will be able to lift up "his countenance".

God's last statement is no longer a rhetorical question, but rather a stern warning. Here is the first mention of the word "sin" in the Bible, from a Hebrew word meaning "missing the mark". Here is also an inference that carnivory must have already begun among the animals, since the imagery is of a predator crouching in wait for its prey. The phrasing of the consequences echoes God's judgment on Eve, the parallelism being that Cain must rule over sin in the same manner as man must rule over woman, even though her desire is to rule him.

But Cain evidently doesn't listen, or even acknowledge God's warning; just sullen silence. We can assume he is already plotting his revenge. Note how easy it now was for a human to commit the worst possible sin against another human. No need for Satan to disguise himself as an animal and tempt Cain to sin. His tendency to sin is already present in his very *nature*. What we now refer to as one's *mind*, the Bible often refers to as *heart*, and repeatedly tells us that man's heart/mind is "more deceitful than all else" and "desperately wicked" (Jer 17:9). Jesus taught that the sin of murder begins in the heart with anger (Matt 5: 20-22). In American jurisprudence, premeditation elevates a crime, especially murder, to warrant the most severe penalty. Again, we see *consistency* in the Creation Model: *internal* consistency from Genesis to the prophets to the gospels, and *external* consistency with regard to our system of justice. The fact that the Evolution Model does not even address this tendency toward sin reveals the Creation Model to be the superior of the two, in that it explains more of the total human experience – not just origins and change over time.

Gen 4: 8 – 15

Hopefully you don't need a spoiler alert to know that Cain murders his brother Abel. The conversation that ensues between him and God is informative. As He did with Adam and Eve, God asks Cain a question to which He already knows the answer. While Adam and Eve gave evasive answers and attempted to shift blame, Cain utters the first outright (human) lie[417], claiming he does not know where his brother is, and then compounding his lie with a defiant question as to whether he should be his brother's keeper. The opportunity for repentance and confession is immediately passed, and God renders judgment without delay. Cain will have to become a vagrant because he will be cursed from the ground, which itself had been cursed by God following the Fall.

While complaining that his punishment is too severe, Cain expresses an interesting fear: that in his wanderings there will be many people who want to kill him. At this point in the narrative, the casual reader might ask, "What people?", since so far, we only have three surviving humans named: Adam, Eve and Cain. We will see the answer in the discussion of the next passage.

Gen 4: 16 – 17 *Then Cain went out from the presence of the Lord, and settled [dwelt] in the land of Nod east of Eden. And Cain had relations with his wife and she conceived, and gave birth to Enoch; and he built a city, and called the name of the city Enoch, after the name of his son.*

The statement that Cain "went out from the presence of the Lord" lends credence to the idea that the early humans continued to communicate with God at the gate of Eden where God's Shekinah Glory was. As mentioned earlier, neither the Creation nor the Evolution Model would predict any surviving evidence of such a place. Also, the Hebrew word *nod* means "wandering", so that the verb "dwelt" is probably more descriptive than "settled", since Cain would still be wandering from place to place.

The Big Question: Where did Cain get his wife[421ff]? This is related to the previous question about "what people?" would want to kill Cain. It is said by many that the misnamed Scopes Monkey Trial pivoted on the great Christian orator William Jennings Bryan being unable to answer this question posed by Clarence Darrow. The answer is simple: Cain, as well as Abel, married their sisters (or possibly nieces or grand-nieces)! I'll pause while you pick yourselves up off the floor!

When you think about it, how could it be otherwise? For the human race to survive after starting with Adam and Eve, siblings or close relatives would have to marry. In the next chapter of Genesis, we will see that at this point mankind has been on the earth about 130 years, and that Adam and Eve had "other sons and daughters" (Gen 5:4). At normal reproduction rates for genetically perfect (or near perfect) humans, there could easily be hundreds of people. The descendants of Abel would be the people Cain feared would try to kill him in revenge for killing their patriarch. Also, there is a common misperception that Cain married a woman he met in the land of Nod, but Bible scholars are in nearly total agreement that Cain was already married and his wife accompanied him by faith.

Today the arguments against marrying a close relative run along two lines of reasoning: one biological and one moral.

Biologically there would be no problem with siblings or close relatives marrying, providing that their genomes were "very good"; in other words, no harmful mutations in their genetic codes. This was certainly true of Adam and Eve and their children. Scientific studies suggest that there would likely have been a much lower rate of mutation in the past, for both humans and animals, because the earth's magnetic field was roughly eight times stronger 6,000 years ago and would shield organisms from much of the harmful radiation that now reaches the surface of the planet. For this reason, it is logical that God would not forbid sibling marriages until another 2,500 years after Cain, during the time of Moses (Lev 18:11). Thus, the Creation Model is logically consistent with both biology and geophysics, while the Evolution Model must invent new hypotheses to explain why Earth's oceans did not boil away a mere 20,000 years ago from the energy of the magnetic field alone[167]!

From a moral standpoint, virtually everyone today has a sense of repugnance about siblings marrying, and this may be a result of the biological reality that marrying a close relative today is likely to result in inherited genetic mutations from both parents. It is odd that this prohibition is nearly universally observed, while others like adultery and homosexuality are widely violated.

Perhaps God has written this prohibition "on our hearts" (Rom 2: 15) in a special way, in addition to forbidding it in His written Law, because he had once condoned the practice, even up to the time of Abraham who married his half-sister. It's not that God changed his mind, but that genetic realities that we couldn't understand at the time (but now do) required Him to "change the rules" for our benefit. It cannot be a coincidence that the science of genetics, developed over the last one hundred years, now provides a complete explanation for why close relatives could marry in the distant past, but can no longer do so safely. The consistency with science was in the Creation Model all along, but had to be incorporated into the Evolution Model decades after Darwin first popularized the model. So, on biological grounds and moral grounds the Creation Model is shown to be superior.

Gen 4: 18 – 24

In this passage, Scripture dispenses with the ungodly line of Cain before turning to the godly line of his younger brother, through whom the promised Seed of the woman will come[429ff]. Murder has already occurred in Cain's line, and within five generations further defiance will come in the person of Lamech, who not only kills a man out of revenge, but also practices polygamy in spite of God's ideal plan of one man and one woman becoming one flesh in a monogamous relationship. Cain's line is characterized by noteworthy technological achievement, with his descendants being credited with city building, development of the nomadic lifestyle (like today's Bedouins), invention of musical instruments, developing metallurgy and manufacturing tools/weapons of brass and iron.

Proponents of the Evolution Model would argue that such technology would not come for many thousands of years after the evolution of man, and only after plodding through a stone age and a period of hunting and gathering before "inventing" agriculture which enabled early man to stay in one place and only then begin to invent things. So which model is best supported by the evidence we find today?

Certainly, we do see evidence of ancient cave dwelling, but even today one can visit a lovely spot in southern Spain where gypsies still live in caves in modern times. Not only that, but we regularly see articles about archeologists and paleontologists continually being "surprised" that the Neanderthals (once thought to be primitive cave-dwelling brutes) actually engaged in tool making, skilled workmanship, art and religious practices[6]. The Creation Model would require these ancient people to be post-Flood people groups, possibly living in caves temporarily to survive the Ice Age, and having to re-invent much technology following their dispersal from Babel. (More on this later.) Evidences that "surprise" evolutionists are predicted by the Creation Model.

The Creation Model also predicts that no evidence of pre-Flood technology would survive a world-wide Flood, so the absence of such evidence agrees with both models. However, evolutionists struggle to explain how early humans could accomplish so much in the areas of astronomy, engineering and construction. Analysis of ancient structures like Stonehenge and the pyramids of Egypt, Asia, South America and Central America show not only advanced skills in quarrying, stone cutting and building, but also a profound knowledge of astronomical cycles. They are surprised (again) by discoveries of ancient sea-faring skills and complex language structure among "primitive" tribes. Creationists, on the other hand, point out that man's skills would have been even more advanced had it not been for the setback caused by God's judgment at Babel. The Creation Model requires no auxiliary hypotheses or special pleading to explain the evidence we find in the present.

Gen 4: 25 – 26 *And Adam had relations with his wife again; and she gave birth to a son, and named him Seth, for she said, "God has appointed me another offspring in place of Abel; for Cain killed him." And to Seth, to him also, a son was born; and he called his name Enosh. Then men began to call upon the name of the Lord.*

Eve's naming of Seth is another word play[439ff], since his name in Hebrew means "appointed". The implication here is that Seth was born not long after Abel's murder. Eve's saving faith in God's promise for a Messiah will be realized in the line of Seth.

The phrase "to call upon the name of the Lord" denotes invocation to God; calling out or proclaiming His name. Scholars consider this to be the beginning of public worship of YHWH, the covenant name of the true God. As mankind dispersed farther and farther from Eden's gate and God's Shekinah Glory, public worship would become the norm, consisting of prayer, praise, and thanksgiving, or in the acknowledgment and celebration of the mercy and help of Jehovah.

Gen 5: 1A *This is the book of the generations of Adam.*

It may seem strange that this half-verse is included with our discussion of Genesis 4. However, we must remember that the Scriptures originally had no chapters or verses. Chapter divisions as we now know them did not appear until the 13th century, although verse divisions appeared about 300 years earlier. As discussed in Message 2, the book of Genesis was compiled as separate historical narratives that were separated – not by chapter and verse – but by *toledot* statements similar to this one. Scholars disagree as to whether a given *toledot* introduces a passage or concludes a passage. I am in no position to judge between my heroes of the faith like Dr. Jonathan Sarfati[17ff] (who believes they introduce a passage) or Dr. Henry Morris II[7] (who believes they conclude a passage). I am inclined to believe that in the early tablets the *toledot* concludes the narrative, but later on it makes more sense that they introduce certain narratives. For this reason, I include this *toledot* as part of the message on Genesis 4.

The important point is not whether these statements introduce or conclude a passage, but that they show how ancient authors indicate that a narrative is *historical*, rather than figurative, mythological or metaphorical. Just as God could be the only One to have firsthand knowledge of the "generations of the heavens and the earth", Adam would be the only human to have firsthand knowledge of these "generations" just recounted. In a modern court of law great weight is given to firsthand testimony from an eyewitness. This *toledot* is unusual in that it mentions "the book of", (the others do not), indicating that these ancient historical accounts were written down, and not just passed on as oral traditions. Likely the Hebrew word *sepher* translated as "book" was a scroll or possibly even a collection of clay tablets. The Creation Model has multiple such testimonies, whereas the Evolution Model can only offer conditional statements with hand-waving by people who were not there, describing things that have never been observed, and professing faith in processes that cannot be repeated. This can hardly be called logical or rational, let alone scientific.

Conclusion

One can sense in these last two messages gathering clouds of gloom. Man's sin against God has gone from simple disobedience of an incredibly simple command, to homicide, lying to one's own omniscient Creator and polygamy in defiance of God's plan for marriage. Man's sin nature is gaining more and more control over him, in spite of God's admonition that we must master it.

And that's the problem. Paul tells us in his letter to the church at Rome that in our natural state, not only are we unable to master sin, but we are slaves to it. Only by making Jesus Christ the Lord and Master of our lives can we ever hope to escape this bondage. "But wait!", you say, "Lord and master sounds like slavery again!"; and indeed, it is. The difference is that we become a "bond slave" or "bond servant" to Christ, which is *voluntary* servitude. In other words, you can choose to remain a slave to sin, or a bond servant to Christ. There is no other option!

Joshua told the Israelites, ". . . choose for yourselves today whom you will serve . . . but as for me and my house, we will serve the Lord." (Josh 24: 15). How about you? Have you made a decision? You may think that you still have time to "think it over", but the fact is: if you haven't made the decision to follow the Lord, **you have automatically chosen the other option.** Don't let that option stand for one more minute. Decide right now to follow the Lord Jesus.

Message 5 – The Seed Line of Seth & the Age of the Earth

. . . and Noah became the father of Shem, Ham and Japheth

TEXT: Genesis 5: 1B – 32

Introduction

After dispensing with the ungodly line of Cain, the historical narrative turns to the Seed line of Seth. Some are tempted to call it the *godly* line of Seth, but this would be a misnomer since only eight members of one family will survive the judgment on the unrighteous that is coming. In keeping with our convention on the *toledot* statements, the half verse that we consider in the opening of this message will be the beginning of Noah's account, having just read the account of Adam.

Many people find the recitation of a long list of generations in Genesis 5 to be tedious, often skipping over the chapter entirely in Bible studies. However, this would be a mistake because it would cause one to overlook two huge elephants in the room:

1. These pre-Flood patriarchs lived to *really* old ages, and
2. The generations come with "date stamps", so that if one were to add up the years in this Chapter, as well as those of Genesis 11, one arrives at a total of 1,056 years from Adam to Noah, and 952 years from Noah to Abraham. Adding the generally accepted value of 2,000 years from Abraham to Christ and 2,000 years from Christ to the present, gives a total age of the creation of something like 6,000 years. [126ff]

Why do I say these are elephants in the room? Quite simply, if one accepts the clear interpretation of the patriarchal ages in Genesis, then *the Evolution Model cannot be true*. The Evolution Model requires 4.5 *billion* years as the age of the earth, and in fact probability studies of chemical evolution scenarios show even that isn't enough time. Since there are only two models, that would leave only the Creation Model as the proper interpretation of the evidence in the world today.

As we work through this chapter, we will discuss how the tools of science can allow us to conclude whether the evidence we see today tends to support – or tends to falsify – the Creation Model.

Genesis 5: 1B – 2 *In the day that God created man, He made him in the likeness of God. He created them male and female, and He blessed them and named them Man [Adam] in the day they were created.*

Here we see a pattern that was begun in Genesis 2 and will be repeated again in 6:9, 10:1 and other passages: a brief summary that ties into what was narrated by the previous author before the *toledot* statement, followed by a more detailed description of first-hand knowledge by the new author.

In Hebrew the word for "man" is *adam*, and here it refers to mankind in general. In other verses (e.g., 4:25) the same Hebrew word is used as a proper name for the first human. Bible translators relied on the context of a given passage to determine which meaning to ascribe to *adam*.

As mentioned in the previous message regarding the significance of the *toledot* statements, the fact that narratives are ascribed to specific authors is further authentication that these are *historical* narratives by real authors who were really there to witness, participate in and record the events. The Evolution Model can offer no such affirmation at any point in the presumed history of that model.

Genesis 5: 3 *When Adam had lived one hundred and thirty years, he became the father of a son and in his own likeness, according to his image, and named him Seth [appointed].*

Before we deal with the skeptic's objection to Adam's advanced age at this point, let's deal with what is perhaps an even more profound objection: "How could Eve still be fertile and able to bear children at 130 years of age?!"[440ff]

For decades scientists have told us that an unborn baby girl is born with all the egg cells that she will ever have, (roughly 7 million) and that they will never be renewed or replenished throughout her life. Furthermore, the number of egg cells is reduced to 1 million at birth which will remain dormant until puberty, by which time the number is down to 300,000 – 400,000. Then they are lost at the rate of 1,000 per month, with only one maturing enough for ovulation. When she runs out of eggs (at what we now call "middle age"), menopause begins. Evolutionists point to this as "scientific proof" that the Bible must be in error, and that God's command to "fill the earth" could not be achieved with women's fertility (not to mention men's) only spanning a few decades.

However, new discoveries published in 2012 have shown the above dogma is mistaken. A number of research teams around the world have demonstrated the existence of *oogonial stem cells* in the ovary, capable of producing a constant supply of fresh eggs, or *oocytes*. This suggests that oogonial stem cells could have played an important role in maintaining Eve's fertility, and in fact these cells would have been functioning much more efficiently than they do today, after thousands of years of mutations caused by the Curse.

So, there is no "scientific proof" that the Bible is in error on this point, but more significant is that there is no such thing as "scientific proof" about anything! Real scientists understand that all scientific conclusions are *tentative*, subject to correction or falsification by subsequent research. So, a prediction of the Evolution Model is falsified by the discovery of oogonial stem cells, but the Creation Model is supported.

One final note about this passage is that it expands upon the naming of Seth described in Gen 4: 25, showing that both Adam and Eve had a role in naming Seth, and that both concurred that God had "appointed" them another son to replace Abel. Their saving faith in God's promise to provide a solution to sin by the Seed of a woman is encouraged by the fact that – unlike Cain – Seth shares Adam's likeness and image and will continue to "call upon the name of the Lord" (Gen 4:26). Unfortunately, like Cain and like each of us, Seth will also pass on the image of Adam's original sin.

Gen 5: 4 – 5 *Then the days of Adam after he became the father of Seth were eight hundred years, and he had other sons and daughters. So all the days that Adam lived were nine hundred and thirty years, and he died.*

Biblical skeptics were doubtful about the previous verse and Adam's age of 130 years, but with these two verses they become absolutely apoplectic! Who ever heard of humans living hundreds and hundreds of years?! On the other hand, biblical literalists would counter that 930 years is actually a drastically truncated lifespan for Adam, since according to God's original plan for His "very good" creation, Adam should still be alive today! The Evolution Model requires death – death of the unfit accompanied by survival of the fittest – in order for the model to work. The Creation Model describes death as "the enemy" (1Cor 15:26) and something to be conquered by the coming Seed of the woman (Is 25:8).

In defending their model, evolutionists invoke the concept of *uniformitarianism*, the idea that processes and changes observed in the present proceeded at the same rate in the past. Under this paradigm, the thousands of feet of sedimentary rock observed in the geological record accumulated over millions of years, applying the same rate of deposition of sediments that we see today. The concept is often defined by a catchphrase: "the present is the key to the past". Extending their paradigm, evolutionists would point to the average lifespans in modern times being longer compared to those of prior centuries due to better nutrition and advances in medical science. Consequently, early humans should have *shorter* lifespans than modern humans since they lacked the knowledge of nutrition and medicine that we enjoy today.

Clearly if there is no evidence in support of long lifespans in the distant past, the scientific basis of the Creation Model would be undermined, as would the idea of biblical inerrancy. Before we examine the evidence any further, let's see if maybe Adam's lifespan was simply an anomaly due to his perfect created condition, and perhaps lifespans subsequently normalized . . .

Gen 5: 6 – 27 *And Seth lived one hundred and five years and became the father of Enosh. Then Seth lived eight hundred and seven years after he became the father of Enosh, and he had other sons and daughters. So all the days of Seth were nine hundred and twelve years, and he died . . . etc. . . etc.*

In these verses we see a pattern that is repeated over and over, "**A** lived ***x*** years and became the father of **B**. Then **A** lived ***y*** years after he became the father of **B** . . . So all the days of **A** were ***x + y*** years and he died." The one exception in this passage is Enoch, of whom it is not said that "he died", but rather that "And Enoch walked with God, and he was not, for God took him" (5:24) after he had attained the age of 365 years. We must be careful to note that there is no indication of declining lifespans in this passage; in fact, Enoch's son, Methusaleh lived for 969 years, longer than any other patriarch mentioned in the Bible.

Clearly, we are faced with confronting the two elephants in the room mentioned in the introduction to this message:

1. The Bible clearly states that early humans typically lived for hundreds of years.
2. The formula used to describe the patriarchs' ages when the next offspring in the Seed line is born, and the following years to the patriarch's death, leaves no room

for extra years, since *there are no gaps* in the timeline. For this reason, this timeline, as well as the timeline in Gen 11, are called *chronogenealogies*.

Admittedly, even many creationists develop heartburn over these verses and their implication. Some, like Dr. Hugh Ross of the ministry *Reasons to Believe*, have offered explanations that even though gaps are not apparent in the text, there *could* be gaps nonetheless. They point to some minor discrepancies in genealogies in the books of Matthew and Luke, as well as discrepancies in other Bible translations based upon the Greek Septuagint or Samaritan Pentateuch manuscripts as opposed to those based upon the Masoretic texts. However, even if such arguments are accepted, they would amount to no more than one or two thousand additional years; nowhere near what would be required to harmonize with the Evolution Model. Plus, accepting the Greek Septuagint timeline would allow for Methuselah to survive the Flood by 14 years, in clear opposition to what Scripture teaches. Some have even argued that the references are to *months*, not years, however applying this idea would lead to absurd conclusions, such as Methuselah being born when his father, Enoch, was only six![448] Obviously, we must seek a science-based explanation of how early humans could live so long, or admit to a major challenge to the Creation Model.[467ff]

In our discussion of Genesis 2 and the tree of life, we mentioned the discovery of *telomeres* at the ends of our chromosomes that protect them from the genetic corruption commonly called "aging", suggesting that perhaps the fruit of that tree contained certain nutrients that would be of particular benefit to such preservation. In 2009 Elizabeth Blackburn was awarded a Nobel Prize for her discovery of the enzyme *telomerase* that can elongate the telomeres, and could theoretically give cells an unlimited capacity for cell divisions (i.e., "life"). Unfortunately, telomerase is very active in cancer cells, allowing them to divide uncontrollably. One line of cancer cells from a woman who died in 1951 is effectively immortal, still dividing to this day, making them useful for advances in medical research. More efficient operation of telomerase in the past, coupled with fewer harmful mutations as a result of a stronger planetary magnetic field, could easily provide the scientific explanation for longer lifespans for our distant ancestors.

We can find additional evidence from research concerning the opposite phenomenon: premature aging. Hutchinson-Gilford progeria syndrome (HGPS) affects one in 8 million children, causing them to age 5 – 10 times faster than usual. They typically suffer from geriatric symptoms like baldness, cataracts and osteoporosis, dying by the age of 13, usually from heart attack or stroke. Genetic research has found that this disease is caused by a *single point mutation* (from cytosine to thymine) in a gene containing 25,000 base-pairs of nucleobases. The fact that such a minor change in the genetic code can cause a tenfold drop in lifespan is strong evidence in support of the longevities described in the Creation Model, and why we don't observe them in people today.

We will deal further with the second elephant – the "young" age for the earth implied by the Creation Model, in Message 11.

Gen 5: 28 – 29 *And Lamech lived one hundred and eighty-two years, and became the father of a son. Now he called his name Noah [comfort; rest], saying, "This one shall give us rest from our work and from the toil of our hands arising from the ground which the Lord has cursed.*

These verses suggest that Lamech was perhaps a prophet to whom God had given an insight that this particular son was destined to bring relief of some kind to humanity from the curse that Adam's sin had produced. Lamech evidently made the same mistake as Eve, in thinking that his son would be the promised Messiah.

Gen 5: 30 – 32 *Then Lamech lived five hundred and ninety-five years after he became the father of Noah, and he had other sons and daughters. So all the days of Lamech were seven hundred and seventy-seven years, and he died. And Noah was five hundred years old, and Noah became the father of Shem, Ham and Japheth.*

Lamech had the shortest natural lifespan of any of the patriarchs up to this point; in fact, his father outlived him by five years.[457] It is significant to realize that if one plots all the lifespans of this chapter in a timeline, there is a considerable amount of generational overlap that is not obvious from a casual reading of the text[449]. For example, almost all of Adam's descendants on this line would have known him, because he died in Lamech's 56th year. Only Noah could have never known him. The reason this is significant is that the history beginning with Genesis 1:1 (as revealed to Adam by God) all the way through Genesis 4 could have been passed on to Lamech by Adam himself! Thus, the Creation Model is reinforced by the fact that any embellishment or distortion of the true history would be constrained throughout the generations, in that any of the patriarchs could have simply inquired of Adam as to the facts. The Evolution Model suffers in comparison in that *none* of its alleged "facts" were ever "fact-checked" by *anyone* throughout the immense time over which they are supposed to have occurred.

A final note of clarification: the casual reader might assume from the phrasing at the end of this passage that Shem, Ham and Japheth were triplets, all born in Noah's 500th year. In later verses Scripture reveals that Japheth was the eldest of the three, therefore born in Noah's 500th year, with Shem being born two years later. Ham is said to be the youngest. Sadly, Noah's brothers and sisters never made it on board the Ark, and if Noah possibly had "other sons and daughters", they didn't either.

Conclusion

The apostle Peter tells us that Noah was "a preacher of righteousness" (2Pet 2:5), and Hebrews 11:7 describes him as a man of faith. We can only imagine the anguish he must have felt as he preached to the people of his day – including his own family and friends – about the judgment to come, only to have his exhortations tragically fall on deaf ears. And he must have pleaded for years and years as the Ark construction proceeded. All of the scoffers perished, with only seven of Noah's loved ones surviving to repopulate the earth.

What about you? Are you a preacher of righteousness, or are you a scoffer? What will happen to your loved ones when the Day of Judgment comes. The apostle Paul tells us in his letter to the church at Rome that "all have sinned and fall short of the glory of God", and that "the wages of sin is death". Peter tells us that salvation is found only in Jesus Christ, there is no other way (Acts 4:12). When Christ returns it will be too late for the scoffers, and it will be too late to preach to the lost. He warned us that He will come unexpectedly, comparing that moment to the "days of Noah" when everyone was attending to business while ignoring their eternal destiny "until the Flood came and took them all away" (Matt 24: 36-39). God's Holy Spirit is calling to you, pleading with you right now. Don't let another moment go by while you risk your eternal salvation, or that of a loved one.

Message 6 – The Ungodly Multiply; Judgment Looms

Then the Lord saw that the wickedness of man was great on the earth . . .

TEXT: Genesis 6: 1 – 22

Introduction

God had commanded Adam and Eve to multiply [1:28]. With each man and woman in prime health and enjoying hundreds of years of parental productivity, the earth could have well been "filled" in the 1,656 years since the creation. Dr. Henry Morris calculated that at a growth rate of only 2% per year (compared to today's rate of a little over 1%), the world's population could have exceeded *10 trillion* people. We must certainly allow for many death's due to warfare and murder as a result of man's increasing wickedness, but a population of many hundreds of millions is not unreasonable to assume, or even several billion. The problem is not that there are too many people, but that there are too few *godly* people. The natural inclination of mankind to sin was only part of the problem. The other part of the problem was some direct intervention by Satan's demons to corrupt the very genome of mankind.

Genesis 6: 1 – 2 *Now it came about, when men began to multiply on the face of the land, and daughters were born to them, that the sons of God saw that the daughters of men were beautiful, and they took wives for themselves, whomever they chose.*

A widely debated question among biblical scholars is, "Who were these 'sons of God'?" Some have tried to equate the sons of God to the godly line of Seth, but this explanation fails on several points that we will not discuss here. The most logical explanation is that in the Old Testament, the term "sons of God" refers to angels. In the New Testament epistles, the term is used to refer to believing Christians, which is a source for much of the confusion on this point. The first five chapters of Genesis do not have the information needed to answer the question as to the identity of these sons of God, so we must apply the tools of exegesis, using Scripture to interpret Scripture. Other OT passages in Job, Daniel and Psalms use the phrase to clearly describe the heavenly beings we call angels. We would infer that these are the fallen angels, the angels that rebelled along with Lucifer (Satan) and were banished to earth. We have to piece this narrative together from Ezekiel 28: 11-19, Revelation 12:4, 2Peter 2:4 and Jude 6-7.

If these "sons of God" are indeed fallen angels, then we are faced with a dilemma. The purpose of this series of messages is to use the ordinary tools of science to analyze two competing theoretical models; to determine whether the Creation Model or the Evolution Model is better supported by the evidence. Unfortunately, science cannot investigate spiritual things like angels. However, perhaps we can use reason and what we know to be true about human genetics and anthropology to determine if this account in Genesis 6 is at least *internally consistent* with other passages of Scripture, and *externally consistent* with what modern science reveals to us.

Another debate concerns the taking of wives by these demons / fallen angels. Some scholars like Dr. Henry Morris interpret this to mean that women (an alternate translation of "wives") were becoming demon-possessed and having promiscuous sex with demon-possessed men[9]. Other scholars like Dr. Jonathan Sarfati contend that the fallen angels were actually inter-marrying with human women and producing offspring[475ff]. We cannot rule out this possibility on scientific grounds, because it is clear in other passages of Scripture [Gen 18 e.g.] that angels can take on the appearance of men and physically eat material food, meaning they must have had physiological features and digestive organs to enable this to happen. Therefore, it is not a stretch to infer they might also have had reproductive organs. Also, in the Bible, angels only appear in human form as men, which explains why this passage explicitly refers to "sons" of God and "daughters" of men.

Genesis 6:3 *Then the Lord said, "My Spirit shall not strive [abide] with man forever, because he also is flesh; nevertheless his days shall be one hundred and twenty years."*

This verse has been interpreted by some as a judgment by God limiting man's lifespan to just 120 years. This cannot be the case, however since Genesis reports following this declaration many lifespans greatly exceeding 120 years. While it does seem to approximately apply as an upper limit today, there are exceptions; such as the French woman Jeanne Louise Calment who lived from 2/21/1875 to 8/4/1997 (122 years and 164 days.)[481] The prevailing view among most scholars is that God is providing a grace period of 120 years before the coming judgment.

Genesis 6: 4 *The Nephilim were on the earth in those days, and also afterward, when the sons of God came in to the daughters of men, and they bore children to them. Those were the mighty men who were of old, men of renown.*

The Hebrew word *nephilim* means "fallen ones", and here seems to apply to the progeny of the fallen angels and human women. The King James Bible and other translations render this word as "giants", based upon the use of the Greek word *gigantes* in the Septuagint. However, Dr. Sarfati and others claim this usage is based upon misinterpretation of the derivation of the Greek word and misapplication of Greek mythology[483ff]. Whatever the true nature of these offspring, it is clear that the human genome was now corrupted, not just by natural sin, but by supernatural intervention into the gene pool.

From a scientific viewpoint there would now be only one way to "fix things": destroy every human with a corrupted genome and preserve the gene pool of the others. But simply preserving the uncorrupted genome was not God's only goal; He also wanted to preserve righteousness (Heb 11:7). So, by this reasoning, having "pure genes" would not save someone who did not also possess a "pure heart".

Genesis 6: 5 – 7

These verses describe God's observation, sorrow and grief at man's wickedness spreading on the earth, and His resolve to "fix things".

Genesis 6: 8 – 9A *But Noah found favor in the eyes of the Lord. These are the records of the generations of Noah.*

In keeping with our methodology of treating the records of Genesis as historical tablets, or *toledots*, with editorial comments occasionally sprinkled in by Moses, this verse and half-verse comprise Noah's closing signature of his tablet, begun in Gen 5:1. Notice that Noah makes no boastful claims about his own righteousness, but modestly states that he "found favor with God". The Hebrew word translated as "favor" is *chen*, also translated as "grace". This is the first mention of grace in the Bible. The first mention of grace in the New Testament is Luke 1:30, where Mary found "favor" (same word as "grace") with God. God's grace is found – not earned.

Genesis 6: 9B – 10 *Noah was a righteous man, blameless in his time. Noah walked with God. And Noah became the father of three sons, Shem, Ham and Japheth.*

So begins the *toledot* compiled by Noah's sons. It is hard to overlook their pride in their father's character in this brief description, which is a marvelous contrast with Noah's own modest description of himself in our previous passage. We will continue to see evidence of Noah's righteousness and blamelessness in this chapter and the next, as he faithfully executes all of God's commands, without question or objection. In fact, there is not even one recorded word from Noah until we get to the end of Chapter 9.

Genesis 6: 11 – 13 *Now the earth was corrupt in the sight of God, and the earth was filled with violence. And God looked on the earth, and behold, it was corrupt; for all flesh had corrupted their way upon the earth. Then God said to Noah, "The end of all flesh has come before Me; for the earth is filled with violence because of them; and behold, I am about to destroy them with the earth.*

The previous *toledot* explained the evil intermarriage between fallen angels and human women, and the tyrannical *Nephilim* who were their offspring. This *toledot* explains the outcome.

Genesis 6: 14 – 17 In these verses God gives explicit instructions to Noah about His design for a vessel to preserve representative kinds of land vertebrates, including mankind. For a thorough scientific treatment of this passage, I would refer you to *Noah's Ark: A Feasibility Study*, by John Woodmorappe[10]. In this brief summary we will examine the scientific underpinnings that provide supporting evidence that God was indeed the Designer[494ff].

- Build an ark – The Hebrew word is *tebah*, and is used only to describe this vessel, as well as the much smaller safety vessel that infant Moses was placed in [Ex 2:3-5]. The Ark of the Covenant is actually a different Hebrew word.
- Build it of gopher wood – The word gopher is actually a transliteration of the same word in Hebrew, and is only found here in Scripture. Scholars can only guess as to what wood this was. Some have suggested cypress or teak, both of which can resist salt water, even if unfinished. Interestingly, the Chinese had a technique of burying teak in the ground to make it even harder (ground? gopher?).
- Make the ark with rooms – The Hebrew word literally means "nests", although we might think of these as "stalls". We can look to low-tech means of housing animals that farmers

have used for centuries to glean what these stalls may have resembled. The Dutch *postall* allows animal wastes to pile up, while the farmer keeps adding straw to cover it. Adding sawdust, shavings or peat moss reduces moisture content and suppresses odor over the long winter. Other ancient techniques include *grupstal* (gutters), sloped or slatted floors, and vermicomposting, all of which would allow a very few people to attend to many animals in a nearly-hibernating state.

- Cover it inside and out with pitch – The Hebrew term translated as pitch means "covering", and is also translated as "atonement". The normal word for pitch (*zephet*) is not used here, so this covering could be similar to the gum or pitch Europeans have made for centuries from pine resin mixed with charcoal. The usual assumption is that God's purpose was for waterproofing, but recent research shows that a resinous coating on both sides of a wall also provides strong impact resistance (like a pickup truck bedliner).
- Length: 300 cubits, Breadth: 50 cubits, Height: 30 cubits – The ancient cubit was the distance from a man's fingers to his elbow, and can range from 18" (standard cubit), to 20.4 " (Sumerian cubit), to 20.6 – 20.8" (Egyptian cubit). Using even the smallest of these measures, the ark would have been the size of a modern ocean liner (450 ft x 75 ft x 45 ft). This would give the ark the volume equivalent to over 340 livestock semi-trailers and could contain 102,000 sheep-sized animals, or 19,000 if each animal was allotted the recommended 0.5 sq meter of area. Note that the actual accommodation is much greater, since the median size of all animals would have been that of a small rat, and most animals could be housed in stackable cages, needing less than half of the ark's available floor space.

  It is also significant that the dimensions of the ark have been shown by naval architects to be an ideal combination for stability and comfort. River barges are built to the same proportions and have proven almost impossible to capsize. Engineering studies have shown that the ark's shape would tend to keep it pointed into the wave direction, generally experiencing less than 3 degrees of tilt.

  Furthermore, we know of ancient wooden ships that were of comparable size to the ark, proving that the skills to build a vessel of this size could have easily existed in Noah's time. The *Leontifera* of Heraclea was 400-500 ft long and performed admirably in an Aegean Sea battle in 280 BC. Chinese admiral Zheng He (or Cheng Ho, 1371-1433) had 9-masted ships that were 400-500 ft long. Additional research has shown that the ancients used a more rigid and leak-proof hull design called *monocoque* (French for "single shell), where the external skin provides the structural support. Other ancient techniques that could have been employed include *mortise and tenon* joints and cross-planking.
- Make a window – The Hebrew word is *tsohar*, and is only used here in Scripture. From its description it seems to be a sheltered opening one cubit high all along the middle of the roof. Architects today employ a similar design, called "clerestory windows" to allow

light into a room, and many factories, warehouses and barns employ the same idea for ventilation. Another important function that this window would have provided on the ark was to dissipate excess animal heat.

- One door – From a structural standpoint, the fewer doors in an ocean-going vessel, the better. From a theological standpoint, the door is a type of the Messiah Jesus, who described Himself as the "door" to eternal life – the only way in. [John 10:9]
- Three decks – If each deck was the same height, then each would have been 10 cubits, or 15 ft high. This would give more than enough headroom for juvenile giraffes and dinosaurs. It would be counterproductive to take mature adult animals on board, since God intended for the animals to be at their maximum reproductive capacity when they disembarked. Also, as already mentioned, stackable cages for the smaller animals, with food stored in overhead bins or mangers, would have made for efficient use of space. For optimum sea-keeping, the largest and most massive animals would have been housed on the lowest deck.

The clear evidence of design in God's instructions for building the ark strongly supports the Creation Model as depicted in the Judeo-Christian Bible. Other ancient accounts of a great flood describe a large vessel to save living things, but they are lacking any scientific rigor. For example, ancient tablets found while excavating the Assyrian capital of Nineveh tell the story of a sort of Babylonian Noah who built a huge boat in the shape of a *cube* – hardly a seaworthy design! Proponents of the Evolution Model deny a worldwide flood, or at most allow for an exaggerated account of a local Mesopotamian flood. But that doesn't explain why there are *thousands* of such stories from all around the world – from the Pawnee tribe in Nebraska, to the Miao tribe in southwest China, to the Aborigines of Australia, to the jungles of the Amazon. To a reasonable person analyzing the totality of these facts, the biblical account of the flood gives the most engineering detail consistent with sound scientific principles.

Genesis 6: 17 -18

In this passage God reveals to Noah the means by which He intends to carry out his decision to "blot out" (or "wipe off") man from the earth – by a "flood of water". The Hebrew word *mabbul*, or the Greek word *kataklysmos* in the Septuagint, are the only terms used to describe the coming cataclysm. Other words are used in Nahum, Psalms or Luke to describe ordinary, local floods. He further reveals that He will destroy "all flesh in which is the breath of life", which would include all land vertebrates, including birds, but would not include sea creatures, microorganisms, insects, or other arthropods. Although billions of these would die (as indicated by the fossil record we have today), some remnant of most of these would survive. God promises to establish His covenant with Noah, but sadly, in verse 18 God informs Noah that only he, his wife, his three sons, and his three daughters-in-law would survive from the entire human race. We know that Noah had brothers and sisters from Gen 5:30, and we can assume he had other sons and daughters from the first 500 years of his life, but they are all to perish with the rest of the wicked.

Genesis 6: 19 – 21 *And of every living thing of all flesh, you shall bring two of every kind into the ark, to keep them alive with you; they shall be male and female. Of the birds after their kind, and of the animals after their kind, of every creeping thing of the ground after its kind, two of every kind shall come to you to keep them alive. And as for you, take for yourself some of all food which is edible, and gather it to yourself; and it shall be for food for you and for them.*

From information we will gain in Gen 11:10, two years after the flood Shem was 100 years old. Noah's three surviving sons were born shortly after he turned 500, and the flood came in his 600th year. Since his sons were already married when God instructed Noah to build the ark, we can deduce that Noah had about 70 years to build the ark and stock it with food for the animals and his family. Although the Bible does not specifically say so, it is reasonable to assume that Noah, who "found favor with God", was probably also blessed with material wealth, which would enable him to hire carpenters and shipwrights to construct presumably the largest structure known to the world at that time. Power tools are not a necessity given enough time, labor and resources to accomplish the job. Even today, Brazilian ship builders using nothing but simple hand tools have crafted exquisite replicas of Columbus's sailing ships that tour coastal ports and attract visitors by the thousands. The fit and finish of these ships rival the craftsmanship of any modern woodworking facility.

Notice that Noah did not have to go out and collect the animals, since God said they "shall come to you". This is not as far-fetched as some critics would have you believe, since even to this day many animals are pre-programmed to undertake vast migrations, often over thousands of miles. We can assume that if animal caretakers were needed once the animals began to assemble, Noah could have afforded them as well.

Genesis 6: 22 *Thus Noah did; according to all that God had commanded him, so he did.*

It is no wonder that the writer of Hebrews includes Noah in the Chapter 11 "Hall of Faith", whom "being warned by God about things not yet seen, in reverence prepared an ark for the salvation of his household . . ." Since Peter referred to Noah as a "preacher of righteousness" [2Pet 2:5] we can imagine the scoffers of his time not only ignoring his pleadings that they repent, but ridiculing him unmercifully for pursuing his folly of an ark. The Bible records no words of protest nor hesitancy on the part of Noah in carrying out God's commands, despite the toll it must have taken on him, his family and his resources. No doubt Noah had to rely extensively on God's support in carrying out such a Herculean task, but we can be confident that the same divine support is accessible to us when we are giving our utmost for Him.

Conclusion

Just as the wicked culture of Noah's day faced an impending judgment, so does our wicked culture today. Paul told the men of Athens in Acts 17, "He has fixed a day in which He will judge the world in righteousness through a Man whom He has appointed, having furnished proof to all men by raising Him from the dead."

How confident are you that if that judgment day were to happen tomorrow, you would be allowed to join our Lord in Heaven? Jesus taught that when that day comes it will be "just like the days of Noah. For as in those days which were before the flood they were eating and drinking, they were marrying and giving in marriage, until the day that Noah entered the ark, and they did not understand until the flood came and took them all away; so shall the coming of the Son of Man be." [Mat 24: 37-39] Just as the ark had only one way in, so Jesus has told us, "I am the way, and the truth, and the life; no one comes to the Father, but through Me."[John 14:6]

Once the day of judgment comes, it's too late. Why not decide right now that you choose eternal life with Jesus?

Message 7 – The Ark is Entered; the Earth is Flooded

And the water prevailed upon the earth one hundred and fifty days

TEXT: Genesis 7: 1 – 24

Introduction

The Bible's account of the Flood is one of the most attacked parts of Scripture. A straightforward reading of the text, and the traditional view of the Church, is clearly a global and universal cataclysm that "blotted out" (or "wiped off") every living thing on the planet. Many modern church leaders attempt to accommodate the secular geologists who cling to the concept of *uniformitarianism* – i.e., the evidence of the global rock record can be explained by the slow and gradual processes we see occurring today (erosion, sedimentation, tectonic plate motion, etc.) continuing over eons of deep time. In so doing, these church leaders have incorporated parts of the Evolution Model into the Creation Model, hoping to appear more "scientific" by allowing for a "tranquil flood", or a local flood confined to only the Mesopotamian region. However, if the Creation Model is true, it must be based firmly on what Scripture clearly states in the original Hebrew language. Both theoretical models have the same evidence: a geologic lithosphere divided up into tectonic plates, continents covered predominately by a mile of sedimentary rock (rock formed from sediments that settled out of water), and billions of dead things buried in rock layers laid down by water all over the earth (fossils). We can use the tools of science to probe this evidence and devise additional explanatory models. Not surprisingly, creationists are not in full agreement as to the detailed chronology of the Flood, since Scripture is silent on many of these details. In this discussion we will focus on the Flood model that appears to have the broadest explanatory support among creation scientists, and contrast that model with the secularist explanation for the same data.

Genesis 7: 1 – 3

After a period of approximately 70 years, the ark is complete, the animals are assembled (by God), and Noah has done all God has commanded him to do. In these three verses God instructs Noah to commence the boarding of animals, with an additional detail that he is to board *seven* mating pairs of the "clean animals". In this context, "clean" must refer to being ritually clean for sacrifice, since divine approval for eating animals has not yet been given. While Moses does not officially define "clean" versus "unclean" animals for us until the books of Leviticus and Deuteronomy, clearly Noah knew what God meant. Only Noah's immediate "household" will comprise the human cargo. We know from Genesis 5 that Noah's father, Lamech, had passed away five years earlier, and his grandfather, Methuselah, had only just died, sparing these righteous patriarchs from the coming calamity.

Genesis 7: 4 *"For after seven more days I will send rain on the earth forty days and forty nights; and I will blot out [wipe off] from the face of the land every living thing that I have made."*

Critics have claimed that seven days would have been insufficient time to board all the animals, but in his book, *Noah's Ark: A Feasibility Study*,[10] John Woodmorappe calculates from modern rates of animal loading that this task could have been accomplished in less than a day. Remember, God only needed to bring a breeding pair (or pairs) from each representative *kind* of animals, (i.e., the taxonomic level of family, or even higher), which Woodmorappe estimates to be around 16,000 individuals, even with very generous assumptions allowed to the critics. Presumably the same docile instinct that God used to bring the animals to the ark location governed the way they would have calmly boarded even such an unfamiliar vessel as the ark, since we are told in verse 9 they "went in".

Critics also point out, correctly, that a worldwide rain lasting forty days is impossible under present meteorological conditions. Dr. Henry Morris's early Flood model postulated a global atmospheric vapor canopy that condensed and collapsed onto the earth, resulting in the forty days of rain[11]. However, more recent calculations have shown that the "greenhouse effect" from a canopy holding that much water would have cooked the earth.[160] While Dr. Morris's model was sound on biblical grounds, it was found to suffer on scientific principles. Like all man-made scientific theoretical models, we should not cling to any theory too tightly, since all science is tentative. At the same time, we should not be too hasty to embrace divine miracles as an explanation, because the prevailing paradigm in Scripture is that of God mostly using natural processes to accomplish His will. Unless a phenomenon is explicitly depicted as a divine miracle (e.g., the feeding of the 5,000 or the Resurrection), we should defer to what appears to be a divine preference for using natural means. For example, God used the natural means of a man-made ark rather than miraculously levitating or re-creating the animal kinds. As will be seen, He used water sources that already existed to cause the Flood and to abate it, and Noah used natural means to decide when it would be safe to leave the ark[535]. In our discussion to come, we will use a preferred Flood model called "catastrophic plate tectonics" to provide a scientific explanation that helps elucidate the teachings of Scripture[531ff].

Genesis 7: 5 – 10

These verses assert for the second time that "Noah did according to all that the Lord had commanded him" and loaded the ark during the allotted seven days.

Genesis 7: 11 - 12 *In the six hundredth year of Noah's life, in the second month, on the seventeenth day of the month. on the same day all the fountains of the great deep burst open, and the floodgates of the sky were opened. And the rain fell upon the earth for forty days and forty nights.*

In teaching my students about the mechanism by which God flooded the earth, I used to refer to this as the "convenience store" verse to give them a memory device (Get it? Seven-Eleven?) In verse 4 above, God told Noah what to expect from *Noah's* perspective (forty days and nights of rain). One would need *God's* perspective to know the true mechanism of the Flood – the breaking up of the fountains of the great deep. Knowing that this was the primary source of water for the Flood helps us to refine the Creation Model using modern observational science coupled with principles of physics, meteorology, hydraulics, thermodynamics, logic and reason.

Even today, some scientists theorize that there is several times as much water in the earth's crust than is in the oceans[12]. Genesis 2:6 describes a mist that rose out of the ground to water the earth, implying that subterranean water under pressure was a source for plant irrigation, as well as a source for the four rivers that flowed from Eden's (presumably) elevated location. Genesis 7:11 seems to imply that a sudden release of this water initiated the Flood. For this to happen, there would need to be widespread rupturing of the earth's crust, and we in fact see evidence for that in the 60,000 km of seafloor spreading zones forming what we now call the mid-ocean ridges[533]. These ridges continue to spew magma and water from the earth's mantle to this day, and even rise above sea level in Iceland to be in full view of airline passengers.

The rupturing and fracturing of the earth's crust would explain the breakup of the pre-Flood land mass into the continents we have today, as well as the forty days and nights of rain. Superheated magma and steam from the mantle would create gigantic jets of water vapor all along the length of the spreading ridge system. These "fountains of the great deep" would then aggregate in the atmosphere and fall back to the surface as intense global rain (the floodgates of the sky were opened). The Hebrew word *geshem* indicates a pouring rain, as opposed to *matar*, a normal rain[557].

The breakup of the earth's original land mass is addressed by secular theoretical models, as well. These models invoke plate tectonics theory, but in a slow, uniformitarian scenario where the crustal plates have always moved at the rate we see today (basically the rate at which your fingernails grow). The mantra of uniformitarian geology is "the present is the key to the past". The Creation Model stipulates that most of the plate movement occurred during the year of the Flood, with today's movement being a small remnant of that original motion. Dr. John Baumgardner has produced a highly regarded computer model that shows how cool coastal rock masses, originally oceanic plates in a state of unstable equilibrium, could catastrophically plunge into the mantle below the less dense continental rock in a process called *runaway subduction*, upsetting the original isostatic balance and pushing the oceans up onto the continents. Evidence for Baumgardner's model is seen in seismic studies that show huge masses of rock in the upper mantle that are cooler than the surrounding mantle material. These must have subducted recently, because if the subduction was over millions of years according to the secular theory, the rock masses would have long ago warmed to the temperature of their molten environment.

The Bible is silent on what the triggering mechanism was that resulted in the fracturing of the earth's crust, and both the secular models and the Creation model require one. Both camps have suggested that a non-miraculous trigger might have been a bombardment by meteors from space, and there is physical evidence for meteoric bombardment in the past. Some creationists have proposed a related theory of an accelerated rate of nuclear radioactive decay preceding the Flood, which would explain not only the triggering mechanism, but also the long ages of rocks calculated from radiometric dating methods.[13] We will look at that theory in more detail when we get to Genesis 11.

Genesis 7: 13 – 16

These verses confirm for the third time that Noah did "as God had commanded him", and his family and the animals were safely aboard and ready for what was to come. In a profound statement, verse 16 concludes with, "and the Lord closed [the door] behind him." From this point on, humans and land animals outside the ark were doomed. Biblical scholar Herbert Carl Leupold suggests that this was a gracious act by *Yahweh* to guard Noah "against possible assaults of the wicked, as well as preventing him from attempting to show ill-timed mercy to last minute penitents."[557]

Genesis 7: 17 – 23

These verses completely rule out the possibility of a local flood, as some modern scholars have tried to assert. Verses 17 and 18 say the Flood continued to increase beyond the first forty days, implying that the subterranean pressures were no longer sending jets of water and vapor high into the atmosphere, but that the fractures in the earth's crust were still disgorging enormous quantities of water. Verse 19 describes the waters continuing to rise to cover the high mountains (though current evidence suggests the highest mountains we see today rose up after the initial stages of the flood, since even Mt. Everest has limestone containing marine fossils called crinoids). Verse 20 continues with the statement that the water rose to a point 15 cubits (22-1/2 ft) higher than the highest mountains, assuring that the ark would not run aground on a submerged mountaintop. Verses 21 thru 23 leave no doubt that "*of all that was on the dry land, all in whose nostrils was the breath of the spirit of life, died.*" The passage specifically includes birds, but would not include microbes, insects or other arthropods since they do not have the "breath of life" nor "nostrils", with the implication that some remnant of these creatures could survive outside the ark on floating vegetation mats or floating carcasses.

An obvious question for even the most casual observer is, "How could all this have happened without leaving evidence?" The obvious answer is, "It couldn't!" So what evidence is there for a global, catastrophic, cataclysmic flood?

- Sedimentary rock formations that extend across vast sections of continents, like the chalk beds seen in the White Cliffs of Dover, England, across Europe into the Middle East, and across the Atlantic into the Austin Chalk of Texas.[538]
- Rapidly buried fossils – For a fossil of a living animal to form it must be quickly buried before decay and scavengers can destroy it. We see fossils of animals caught in the act of swallowing their lunch, giving birth, fighting, struggling for breath, and fleeing rising waters. We see land animals like dinosaurs buried with sea creatures. We see clams by the millions buried while alive (i.e., shells are closed).[539]
- Evidence that multiple rock layers were laid down simultaneously, such as fossilized trees transecting different rock layers claimed by secular scientists to have formed over timespans of millions of years. This can be confirmed by experimental science performed in flume studies such as those published by Dr. Guy Berthault.[544]
- Massive erosion over thousands of square miles as seen in the American southwest mesas and formations like Devil's Tower in Wyoming.[547]

- Planation surfaces, water gaps and rapidly formed canyons that can only be logically explained by the receding stages of a massive flood (sheet flow followed by channelized flow).[548]
- Evidence of high-speed currents causing cavitation and erosion of tremendous boulders, followed by transport over thousands of miles (e.g., Appalachia to southwest USA). [541]

Even secular scientists have now begun to reluctantly admit that many of these structures had to have been formed catastrophically. Though most of them still refuse to acknowledge a global flood, they have come to be known as "neo-catastrophists", as more and more of them are discarding the obviously false geologic theme of uniformitarianism.
To any fair-minded person, the Creation Model and the Flood provide the best explanation for geologic formations observed all over the world. The Evolution Model and its associated concept of uniformitarianism falls woefully short of being a scientific explanation.

Genesis 7: 24 *And the water prevailed upon the earth one hundred and fifty days.*
Australian geologist Dr. Tas Walker has published a Flood model based upon the book of Genesis and his own scientific observations over decades of research[536ff]. His model proposes two main stages of the Flood "year" (really 370 days) as the *inundatory stage* and the *recessive stage*. The inundatory stage is further divided into the *eruptive phase* (the bursting forth of the fountains of the great deep), the *ascending phase* (derived from the waters increasing upon the earth), and the *zenithic phase* (derived from the waters having peaked after "prevailing" for so long with the mountains covered). The recessive stage will be described in Genesis 8.

Conclusion
In our culture, most people have not concerned themselves much with the study of the Flood as described in Genesis, let alone with the study of geology or paleontology. For this reason, they pooh-pooh the whole idea of a global flood and a floating zoo, preferring to comfort themselves that "science" and "uniformitarianism" explain the rock record developing over millions of years. The apostle Peter knew these scoffers well, describing them as

> "saying 'Where is the promise of His coming? For ever since the fathers fell asleep, all continues just as it was from the beginning of creation [uniformitarianism – the present is the key to the past].' For when they maintain this, it escapes their notice that by the word of God the heavens existed long ago and the earth was formed out of water and by water, through which the world at that time was destroyed, being flooded with water." [2Pet 3: 5-6]

I am convinced that if everyone would take just an hour or two to watch one of the many video presentations available in the creationist media, they would soon be convinced of the superiority of the Creation model. Many of these videos are available to watch for free on websites such as www.answersingenesis.org or www.creation.com. A good one featuring Dr. Tas Walker is *Biblical Geology – Properly Understanding the Rocks*.

The prophet Hosea lamented, "My people are destroyed for lack of knowledge", and it seems that is what is happening to those in our culture today who refuse to look beyond the evolutionary indoctrination they have been immersed in since grade school. Thousands of people have written in to the various creation ministries exclaiming how their eyes have been opened by some of the teaching they allowed themselves to be exposed to. The physical evidence for the Flood is so apparent all around us that deniers, paraphrasing the apostle Paul, are "without excuse".

What about you? Will the Lord deem you to be "without excuse" on the Day of Judgment merely because you refused to acknowledge the evidence for His judgment in Noah's day? What do you have to lose? If you examine the evidence for a worldwide flood and find it lacking, it has cost you nothing, and you can continue enjoying your Evolution Model. If on the other hand you find, as millions have before you, that the evidence for the Flood is compelling, you stand to gain a reward that is priceless, eternal and has already been purchased for you.

Message 8 – The Flood Recedes

But God remembered Noah

TEXT: Genesis 8: 1 – 22

Introduction

In our discussion of Genesis 7 we mentioned Dr. Tas Walker's Flood model consisting of the *eruptive phase,* the *ascending phase*, and the *zenithic stage*, followed by the *recessive phase.* One hundred, fifty days (including the initial forty) of rain and release of subterranean waters have resulted in the earth being covered fifteen cubits (23 feet) higher than the highest mountains at that time. At some point during that period the water reached its zenith, perhaps remaining there for an indeterminate time, and then began receding. This is where Genesis 8 picks up the narrative.

As before, we will continue to examine the biblical narrative with an eye toward modern scientific observations of geology, meteorology, geography and paleontology to determine whether the evidence best supports the Evolution Model or the Creation Model as the definitive theoretical model of past events.

Genesis 8: 1 *But God remembered Noah and all the beasts and all the cattle that were with him in the ark, and God caused a wind to pass over the earth, and the water subsided.*

The phrase "God remembered" is a Hebrew idiom found elsewhere in Scripture, and does not imply that Noah and the wild and domestic animals were in danger of being forgotten by God[568]. For example, the phrase is used in relation to Abraham's rescue of Lot [Gen 19:29], God's covenant with the patriarchs [Ex 2:24], God's restoration of Israel [Jer2:2], etc. In general, it seems to refer to a promise or covenant previously made being honored at a later time by God.

It would be ridiculous to assume that God sent the wind to "dry up" the water[569]. Rather, this detail might be referring to God establishing the global wind patterns that we observe today due to regions of latitude being unequally heated by the sun, resulting in large convection currents steered by the planet's rotation and the Coriolis effect. Today we refer to these global winds with names like "prevailing westerlies", trade winds, "polar easterlies" and Jet Stream. These global wind patterns serve the purpose of distributing equatorial heat to higher latitudes, without which vast portions of the earth would be uninhabitable, preventing animals from dispersing over the earth to fill it. Another purpose for the wind might have been to counteract the turbulence of the ocean caused by massive eddies called *gyres*, which are also a result of the Coriolis effect acting on vast regions of ocean[565]. Today these gyres are modest because of their interaction with the continents, but unfortunately result in expansive areas of oceans being clogged with floating garbage and debris that are carefully avoided by trans-Atlantic cruise ships. The same effect is seen in the cyclones and hurricanes that mostly rotate counter-clockwise in the northern hemisphere.

Given what we now know about global winds, gyres and cyclones, it is not surprising that the Bible would make mention of the wind that God caused to pass over the whole earth, although in a pre-scientific era this would not have been so obvious. This mention of a global wind provides additional support to the scientific basis of the Creation Model.

Genesis 8: 2 – 5

These verses describe the closing of the "fountains of the great deep", and the cessation of the torrential rains from the "floodgates of the sky", followed by the water receding until the ark "rested upon the mountains of Ararat". This happened exactly five months (using the Hebrew calendar consisting of 30-day months), or 150 days after the initiation of the Flood. Assuming the ark's draught below water was about one-third its height, then the ark found a stable resting position with an even keel ten cubits (fifteen feet) below the surface. The Hebrew word for "rest" is related to the word for Noah, *nuach*, another facet of God's "remembering Noah". Then for 74 more days the water receded until the tops of the mountains around the ark became visible above the water's surface.

Perhaps now is a good time to address the perennial question of the skeptic, "If the Flood really happened, where is all the water now?" The answer is quite simple: it's still here! In his highly regarded book *The Ocean World*, famed oceanographer and atheistic evolutionist Jacques Cousteau states,

> "Were the crust to be leveled – with great mountain ranges like the Himalayas and ocean abysses like the Marianas Trench evened out – no land at all would show above the surface of the sea. Earth would be covered by a uniform sheet of water – more than 10,000 feet deep! The earth is truly a water planet . . . "[14]

So, if the Flood resulted in a smoothed-out planet covered by nearly two miles of water, it stands to reason that for the water to go away, the planet must become *less smooth*[569]. Both secular and creationist geologists agree that the extremely high mountains we see today have been raised up by tectonic plate forces and a principle called *isostacy*, which results in land masses being elevated and ocean basins being lowered. As the water flowed off the land masses, the initial stage would consist of *sheet flow*, resulting in extensive planation surfaces (i.e., planed off flat). There are literally thousands of vistas around the world that display planation surfaces (flat-top mountains). Breeches in these planation surfaces are called water gaps (although many secular geologists who deny a global flood refer to them instead as wind gaps), and these gaps funneled the runoff into *channelized flow*, forming the great canyons we see on every continent, and even offshore of the continents. These types of geologic features all over the world give strong evidential support for the global deluge described in Genesis and for the Creation Model in general.

Another perennial question, from creationists and skeptics alike, is, "Where did the ark land exactly, and is it (or its remnant) still there?" While there exists today a mountain named Ararat in modern Turkey, it is probably a post-Flood volcano[571]. In the Bible, Ararat is a country or region [e.g., 2Kings 19:37], so "the mountains of Ararat" could refer to a large region known to geologists as the Armenian plateau, which even extends into modern Iran. For centuries, even into modern times, there have been reports of sightings of the ark by earlier cultures, and even mysterious images below the ice sheet from modern ground penetrating radar. However, no such claims have been substantiated by subsequent investigation, and the Creation Model takes no stand on this, since the Bible makes no mention of what became of the ark. More than likely, in a post-Flood world denuded of forests, it would have been disassembled and used for building shelters or even for firewood. This is believed to have been the fate of the Pilgrims' *Mayflower*[572].

Genesis 8: 6 – 12

These verses describe Noah's personal investigation into the status of the receding stage of the Flood, since evidently God was not at this point giving him particular instruction[573ff]. His investigation consisted of:

- Waiting 40 more days after the ark came to rest, opening the window (presumably one of the 1-cubit clerestory windows described in Gen 6:16), and releasing a raven. There are valid scientific reasons to release a raven first. They are scavengers and can survive by eating the carrion that must have been in plentiful supply, exposed as bloated carcasses floating on the water or washed up onto the developing shorelines. The exposed mountain tops would provide a raven with resting and nesting spots. The Bible seems to imply that the raven did not return, which would have been an encouraging sign to Noah that the land was drying out. Theologically this could be a "type" of the role ravens would later play in sustaining Elijah [1Kings 17: 4-6].
- Noah subsequently released a dove. Doves do not typically eat carrion, and prefer valleys to mountaintops for nesting. They are powerful fliers, able to cover large ranges, and like dry and clean places for nesting. The dove returned to Noah, having "found no resting place for the sole of her foot".
- After another seven days, Noah again released the dove, which returned to him that evening, but this time with a freshly plucked olive leaf in her beak. This would have further encouraged Noah, since olive trees had begun to sprout. New trees can propagate from olive branches, can tolerate wet, salty or stony ground, and can tolerate a wide pH range. However, while the trees can sprout from wet ground, doves won't nest (or rest) on such a surface, since the trees would not be of sufficient size at this point. The return of the dove signaled to Noah that the ground still needed to dry out more to safely disembark.
- After another week, Noah sent out the dove again, and this time the dove did not return; another encouraging sign that the ground was drying out.

Genesis 8: 13-14

It would be nearly a month later (29 days to be exact) that Noah removes the covering (or roof) of the ark to get a full view of the ground below. While the Bible says that the surface of the ground was dry, Noah could not be sure that it was firm enough beneath the surface to support the weight of the animals. Indeed, it would require another 56 days before God informs Noah by divine revelation that it is safe to unload the animals.

Genesis 8: 15 – 17 *Then God spoke to Noah saying, "Go out of the ark, you and your wife and your sons and your sons' wives with you. Bring out with you every living thing of all flesh that is with you, birds and animals and every creeping thing that creeps on the earth, that they may breed [swarm] abundantly on the earth and be fruitful and multiply on the earth."*

It is not surprising that Noah would have needed direct revelation from God to encourage him to disembark. We can only begin to imagine the changed planet he was presented with:

- As indicated by the olive leaf, what ecologists call *primary succession* would have begun, with grasses and weeds taking root, having been seeded by sprouts and seeds from massive mats of floating vegetation being dispersed by the wind and waves. But no trees, nor edible vegetation would be available for use by Noah's family.
- There would be extremes of weather caused (as they are now) by unequal solar heating of water and land masses producing high winds and precipitation.
- Warm oceans caused by the hot springs and underwater volcanoes characterizing the breaking up of the fountains of the deep (a remnant of which persists to this day) would cause vastly increased surface evaporation. Precipitation over land masses would increase immensely, as confirmed by modern meteorological computer simulations.
- Worldwide climate would cool due to airborne aerosols from prolific volcanic activity resulting from the plate tectonics disturbances continuing after the Flood. This phenomenon is observed today following large volcanic eruptions. For example, the eruption of Mt. Pinatubo in the Philippines in 1991 reduced sunlight worldwide by 10 %, resulting in average global temperatures 0.4 degrees Celsius (0.7 degrees F) cooler over the next two years. Imagine the cumulative effect of thousands of volcanoes over scores, or hundreds, of years!
- Warm oceans, high precipitation and cooler temperatures would result in massive accumulation of snow in the higher latitudes, ushering in an Ice Age that calculations show would last for hundreds of years.
- As ice sheets develop in the higher latitudes, sea levels would drop, exposing land bridges that would allow animals to obey God's command to swarm all over the earth and multiply. Secular scientists agree that sea levels were hundreds of meters lower in the past, and that such land bridges did in fact exist.
- Animals and plants would need genetic information to allow them to adapt to the wide climate variations of tropical jungles, arid deserts and frigid temperatures. More and more genetic research is revealing how such genetic information in animal genomes can be "switched on" in response to environmental stimuli. Such research is also revealing how rapid speciation after the Flood produced the millions of species that we have now

from one (or seven) mating pairs of the original "kinds" that disembarked from the ark[580ff].

- Herbivores would have to forage far and wide to find enough vegetation to survive and multiply, thereby obeying God's command to swarm over the earth.
- Carnivores would initially find plenty of buried carrion to subsist on, as well as fish stranded in shallow pools left by the retreating waters. Even today carnivores that normally hunt often prefer carrion in order to save energy. Thus, assuming Noah was careful in how he released prey and predators from the ark, it would not be necessary for the ark animals to eat one another in order to survive.

Observations in the modern world, as well as paleontological evidence of the world that then was, provide overwhelming support for the Creation Model. In contrast, the Evolution Model, with its principle of uniformitarianism and slow processes over eons of time, cannot account for planed off mountains, thousands of feet of sediments, canyons gorged out of solid rock, nor billions of dead things buried in rock layers laid down by water all over the earth. The evidence cries out, "Lots of water over a short period of time", not "a little bit of water over long periods of time".

Genesis 8: 18 – 20

These verses echo a theme begun in Chapters 6 and 7 when "Noah did according to all that the Lord had commanded him." After he and his family exited the ark, the animals went out "by their families" or "according to their kind". Noah's first act after this more than a year-long ordeal was to worship God by building an altar and making a burnt offering of every clean animal and bird. This is the first mention of an altar in the Bible, which may indicate that since offerings could no longer be offered at the gates to Eden, the new means of sacrifice would be on an altar. Noah's faith is seen in the fact that he sacrificed one-seventh of his breeding stock of clean animals to express his gratitude to the faithful covenant God who brought them through the cataclysm.

Genesis 8: 21-22 *And the Lord smelled the soothing aroma; and the Lord said to Himself [in His heart], "I will never again curse the ground on account of man, for the intent of man's heart is evil from his youth, and I will never again destroy every living thing, as I have done.*

While the earth remains, Seedtime and harvest, And cold and heat,
And summer and winter, and day and night Shall not cease."

It is significant that these verses do not constitute a promise to Noah *per se*, but rather a commitment that God lays upon Himself. His commitment is to never again destroy the ground and its inhabitants as He did with the Flood, and furthermore the solar and seasonal cycles established during the creation week will persist as long as the planet itself does. Note that God is not promising that there will never be "climate change". The persistence of seedtime and harvest does not rule out the possibility of temporary droughts and famines. The persistence of seasons does not rule out the possibility that some summers might be hotter than others, or some winters colder. Days and nights are actually getting longer as the earth's rotation slows ever so slightly, but they shall not cease. The book of Revelation tells us that the earth will not "remain" in its current form forever, but will be replaced with a new heaven and earth; but until then God's commitment to himself (in His heart) will persist.

Note that God's commitment to never again destroy the earth by water rules out the possibility that the Flood of Noah's day could have been local to the Mesopotamian area, as some "long age" or "old earth" theologians have claimed. Clearly there have been thousands of local floods since Noah, which would have been violations of God's commitment if Noah's Flood were merely a local event. God's commitment to Himself will be expanded upon as a formal covenant with mankind in Genesis 9.

Conclusion

God's commitment to never again destroy the earth on account of man is good news, but it comes with some bad news. Because the descendants of Noah will possess the same sin nature as all descendants of Adam, "the intent of man's heart is evil from his youth". A just and righteous God demands judgment on sin and evil. This judgment will not come by way of total destruction of all things, as before, but will come to us individually as sinners. There is nothing we can do individually to escape this judgment, for "all have sinned and fall short of the glory of God." [Rom 3:23].

However, there is good news! Jesus said, "He who hears My word and believes Him who sent Me, has eternal life, and does not come into judgment, but has passed out of death and into life." [John 5:24]. Christians will not see the judgment that is coming to everyone else! That judgment is described in detail in the book of Revelation and involves *severe* climate change, drought, famine, disease, and much more for a time of tribulation.

How does one become a Christian? Just as God made a commitment "in His heart", so you can make such a commitment in yours. Admit you are a helpless sinner, believe that the God who created you became our human savior by sacrificing Himself, and commit to following Him from now on in your earthly life. Your only alternative is to believe in an Evolution Model that pretends we came from nothing, that there are no moral absolutes, and there is no ultimate judgment but merely an uncaring, pitiless universe.

Message 9 – God's Covenant with Noah

And I establish My covenant with you

Text: Genesis 9:1 – 29

Introduction

In Gen 6:18 God promised Noah that He would make a covenant with him. In this passage we see the fulfillment of that promise, the third general, or universal, covenant of the Bible, but the first time the word "covenant" is used. The Edenic Covenant (Gen 2: 15-17) was terminated when Adam and Eve disobeyed God's command not to eat the forbidden fruit. The Adamic Covenant (Gen 3: 14-21) set forth the conditions that will prevail until the curse of sin is lifted. The Noahic Covenant, the first 19 verses of Chapter 9, reaffirms the Adamic Covenant and its dominion mandate, with the addition of the principle of human government to suppress violence and murder. It is unconditional and everlasting (9:16) and applies not just to Noah and his seed (9:9), but also to the animal kingdom (9:10) and even to the earth itself (9:13).

Genesis 9:1 *And God blessed Noah and his sons and said to them, "Be fruitful and multiply, and fill the earth . . ."*

God reaffirms his command of Gen 1:28 and 8:17 to fill the earth. Scripture does not mention any more children being born to Mr. and Mrs. Noah, so the entire human population we see today must have originated with Noah's three sons and their wives. Modern genetic research reveals evidence consistent with the biblical Creation Model, but that is a problem for the secular Evolution Model. Evidence is seen for what scientists call a "genetic bottleneck" resulting in only four human gene pools. Noah's sons would have come from the gene pool of their parents, and each of their wives would account for the other three gene pools (assuming that their wives were not close relatives). Dr. Henry Morris cites calculations that show that these gene pools would have provided far more than enough genetic variation to account for all the wide range of characteristics in present day people groups, and that a population growth rate of merely one-half percent and only 2.5 children per family could easily accomplish the present world population to develop in roughly 4,000 years[17]. Evolutionists, on the other hand, must propose all kinds of tragic scenarios to attempt to explain why the present human population is so small if it has been developing over hundreds of thousands of years.

Genesis 9:2 *"And the fear of you and the terror of you shall be on every beast of the earth and on every bird of the sky; with everything that creeps on the ground, and all the fish of the sea, into your hand they are given . . ."*

The "dominion mandate" of the Edenic Covenant is here re-affirmed, but with an addendum that the wild animals of the earth would from henceforth have a fear and terror of mankind. Note that God does not include "cattle" in this pronouncement, so the inference is that man will still be able to raise domesticated herds and flocks as before. What a far cry from the "very good" pronouncement of Genesis 1:29-31 when all animals and humans were vegetarians. We can see from the fossil record that carnivory was being practiced by animals in the wild prior to the Flood, and presumably came about as part of God's curse upon "the ground" in Gen 3:17. This perhaps explains why God saw it was necessary to instill fear and dread of man, since carnivorous animals would repopulate much faster than humans, and with their superior strength and attack/defense structures might have exterminated the fledgling human remnant. Later, as the human population increased, the reverse might have occurred. With his superior intellect and craftsmanship skills, man was able to hunt the largest of the wild animals (including the great whales of the oceans), driving many of them to near extinction.

Evolutionists, of course, have their own explanation within their theoretical model of how this fear and dread came about, citing "survival of the fittest" coupled with natural selection as the cause of this outcome, resulting in a natural world "red in tooth and claw". However, the Evolution Model then falls short in explaining phenomena such as altruism, observed in both humans and animals, whereas the Creation Model gives a much more coherent and internally consistent narrative.

Genesis 9: 3 – 4 "*Every moving thing that is alive shall be food for you; I give all to you, as I gave the green plant. Only you shall not eat flesh with its life, that is, its blood. . .*"

Here for the first time since the Creation God gives mankind permission to eat meat, in a style parallel to His instruction in Gen 1:29 in which He gave every plant, seed and fruit. Where that instruction had one caveat – not to eat of a particular tree – so this instruction is framed by the caveat to not eat meat with the animal's blood still in it. Note that this is permission – not a mandate – to eat meat. It is entirely possible, although Scripture does not say, that pre-Flood sinful humans had already resorted to eating meat, especially once they saw the carnivorous animals doing it, but a godly man like Noah would not have done so. Two questions arise from this passage: "Why is it necessary to now allow meat eating?", and "Why the restriction about eating meat with blood in it?".

Ecologists study a process called "primary succession", where an ecosystem that is completely destroyed (for example the area surrounding Mt. Saint Helens in Washington state) regenerates itself over time. Grasses and scrub bushes appear quite soon, but it is many years before "plants yielding seed" and "trees bearing fruit" follow in a process called "secondary succession". While grasses and shrubs can provide forage for animals, humans cannot subsist on such fare. Eating meat from creatures higher up the food chain is how humans would be able to acquire a high enough concentration of the nutrients needed to survive, let alone to "multiply and fill the earth". Again, we see observations of modern science revealing more evidence for God's wisdom in His dealings with His creation.

The instruction to abstain from eating of blood appears here, as well as in Deuteronomy and Leviticus, where blood is equated with life. Leviticus 17:11 gives further explanation, "For the life of the flesh is in the blood, and I have given it to you on the altar to make atonement for your souls; for it is the blood by the reason of the life that makes atonement." This in turn is a type of the blood of the Messiah. While the blood of animals would merely *cover* sins, so would need to be offered repeatedly, the blood of the Messiah would *take away* all sins, so this blood would be shed only once.

In addition to the theological significance of equating blood to life in pointing to the atoning sacrifice of the Messiah, modern science has shed further light on how important blood is. As recently as the 19th century, some medical practitioners were still practicing "blood- letting" to rid a patient of an illness believed to have been caused by bad blood. But scientific discoveries beginning in the late 19th century began to reveal how trillions of red blood cells containing hemoglobin are able absorb oxygen in the lungs and transport it to every cell of the body that needs it[600]. Later it was found that blood also carries antibodies and white blood cells to allow the body to cope with a wide range of microbial invaders. Much later in the 20th century the biochemical cascade that results in blood clotting was described. If this remarkable process is not carefully regulated, clotting will occur too easily, or not at all, with fatal consequences either way. Evolutionists are at a loss to explain how such a complicated chemical pathway could have ever arisen by accident, but creationists can point to God's Word which has always recognized the life-sustaining properties of blood.

Genesis 9: 5 – 7 *"And surely I will require your lifeblood; from every beast I will require it. And from every man, from every man's brother I will require the life of man.*

"Whoever sheds man's blood, by man his blood shall be shed,
For in the image of God He made man
And as for you, be fruitful and multiply;
Populate the earth abundantly and multiply in it."

God here institutes capital punishment for murder. Logically, if the blood of animals is considered too sacred to eat, how much more sacred is the blood of man who is made in God's image? If either man or beast slays a man, that man or that animal is judicially ("by man") to be slain himself, the reason being the divine sacredness of human life. The implication is that it is mankind's responsibility to establish human government with the power of capital punishment over society ("every man's brother"), and this mandate has never been revoked. It does not stipulate the form, but only the fact, of government. A logical extension of this mandate would be that this government also enact and enforce regulations against those human activities that might lead to murder if unrestrained (e.g. stealing, adultery).

Only the Judeo-Christian Creation Model gives a logical basis for the sanctity of human life. According to the Evolution Model, survival is for the "fittest", and therefore atrocities like genocide, euthanasia, eugenics and abortion are all acceptable means to arrive at the "fittest", or master race if you will. In the words of Dr. Phil, "How has that been working out for you?"

In repeating for the fourth time His command to "fill the earth", God's wishes for mankind should be abundantly clear. However, as we shall see in Genesis 11, man will once again disobey God by building a tower for permanent settlement at Babel.

Genesis 9: 8 – 11

In these verses God fulfills His promise from Gen 6:18 to make a covenant with Noah, as well as with all future generations of mankind (his descendants/offspring), and all living creatures of the earth for all time. God states His unconditional promise (which He had already "said to Himself" in Gen 8:21) to never again destroy the earth by a flood.

Despite the clear description in Genesis 7 of a global Flood covering "all the high mountains everywhere under the heavens", many skeptics, and even Christian theologians, today claim that the Flood was merely a regional flood in Mesopotamia, enhanced and exaggerated over the millennia in the retelling of the oral history. If that were truly the case, then God has violated His covenant countless times with all the highly destructive local floods and tsunamis that have occurred since this promise was made. Flood sediments, often over a mile thick on every continent, with the same megasequences stretching across continents and across oceans, attest to the fact that a global Flood happened once, and only once, in all of Earth's history.

Genesis 9: 12 – 17

In this passage God establishes the "sign" of His covenant as the rainbow. There is considerable disagreement among scholars as to whether there was such a thing as a rainbow before this time, and in fact whether there was even rain before the Flood.

Theologically, there is no reason to insist that there were no rainbows prior to the Flood just because God established it as a sign of His covenant. God established circumcision as a sign of His covenant with Abraham to make him a great nation (Gen 17:11), but there is no reason to assume that circumcision did not exist until this time. Jesus established the Lord's Supper as a sign of His New Covenant (1 Cor 11: 23-26), but this was certainly not the first time that bread and wine were consumed.

The phrase, "I set My bow in the cloud" in verse 13 has implied to many that the rainbow was not "in the cloud" before God "set" it there. The fact that it would then be a recurring phenomenon is implied by verse 16 where God says, "When the bow is in the cloud, then I will look upon it to remember the everlasting covenant . . ."

Further support for the rainbow being a brand-new phenomenon is gleaned from Genesis 2:5 which says that, " . . . the Lord God had not sent rain upon the earth . . ."; and the following verse describes how the ground was watered by a "mist [that] used to rise from the earth". In fact, rain is not again mentioned until the initiation of the forty days and nights of rain in Genesis 7:12. Without going into a whole lot of technical detail, there is some scientific basis for there being no rainbows prior to the Flood if one assumes a radically different climate then. This is not a huge stretch of the imagination, since fossil evidence suggests that the earth's antediluvian climate was more uniform and conducive to plant growth (coal beds in high latitudes, including Antarctica, for example). Such a climate would result from there being what Dr. Henry Morris described as a "vapor canopy" in the upper atmosphere that would have enhanced the atmospheric greenhouse effect. Carbon dioxide seems to get all the press coverage these days for producing the greenhouse effect - supposedly causing global warming - but water vapor is a much more effective greenhouse gas.

If some sort of vapor canopy existed, it would have the additional effect of diffusing (or scattering) sunlight. This would mean that the sun's rays would not be arriving in the lower atmosphere as parallel rays, even on a "clear" day. But, for a rainbow to be visible across the sky, **parallel** rays must be refracted and reflected within water droplets, and then separated into colors by dispersion.

Since creationist scientists are not in agreement among themselves about Morris's putative vapor canopy, no specific support for the Creation Model can be cited in these verses. Nonetheless, it is interesting to note that the scientific reason *why* there might not have been pre-Flood rainbows was not explained until thousands of years later by Isaac Newton.

Genesis 9: 18 – 19 *Now the sons of Noah who came out of the ark were Shem and Ham and Japheth; and Ham was the father of Canaan. These three were the sons of Noah; and from these the whole earth was populated.*

The renaming of Noah's three sons here, whom we already knew from Gen 6 and 7, is not superfluous, but emphasizes the fact that the whole earth was to be populated from these men and their wives and *only* them. In our discussion of Gen 9:1 we have already seen how today's population could have come from a genetic bottleneck of just these four couples. The other point of these verses is to introduce us to Canaan, the youngest son of Noah's youngest son, and yet the first named grandson in the narrative. In the account that follows, it seems that years – even decades – have passed, since Canaan seems to be "of age".

Genesis 9: 20 – 21

Here we are told of Noah's one recorded moral failure. He became a farmer, planted a vineyard, made wine and got drunk, ultimately passing out naked in his tent. There is no reason to assume that winemaking was not already a developed art in the 1,500 years leading up to Noah, and so it is likely that Noah knew about fermentation and its effects. Making and drinking wine is not in itself sinful[617] , but the Bible is clear that drinking to excess *is*. This actually is strong support for the Creation Model as a true historical account, because unlike virtually all other examples of ancient literature, the Bible doesn't hide the faults of even its greatest heroes (Jesus of course really *was* perfectly sinless). The skeptic who wants to dismiss the biblical account as mythological has to explain why it is so unique in revealing the failings of its principals like, Adam, Noah, Job, Moses, David and even the apostles.

Genesis 9: 22 *And Ham, the father of Canaan, saw the nakedness of his father, and told his two brothers outside.*

Most English translations of this verse do not convey its true sense in the Hebrew. "Saw his father's nakedness" translates the Hebrew *wayyar*, which implies Ham "gazed with satisfaction" at Noah, reveling in his father's shame instead of honoring this godly man who had found so much favor with God[618]. Similarly, "told his brothers" translates the Hebrew *wayyaggehd*, which implies, "told with delight". Dr. Henry Morris suggests, "There was apparently a carnal and rebellious bent to Ham's nature", and Dr. Sarfati offers the conjecture that Noah discerned this same evil had developed to a greater degree in Canaan, and would extend to his descendants[619-621].

Genesis 9: 23 – 24 These verses describe the respectful way in which Ham's two brothers dealt with their father's sad situation, and ends with the statement that when Noah awoke, "he knew what his youngest son had done to him". Note that Ham was no youngster, but was probably around 100 years old, with his youngest son, Canaan, being his fourth son[618].

Genesis 9: 25 – 27 This passage begins with Noah cursing Ham's youngest son, Canaan, which explains why this narrative has repeatedly mentioned "Ham was the father of Canaan." But one might wonder, "Why curse Canaan when Ham was the one who did the evil deed?" We must remember that God had already blessed Ham, along with Noah, Japheth and Seth (Gen 9: 1), and as already mentioned, Noah probably foresaw Ham's inherited rebelliousness in Canaan and his children. The curse specifies that Canaan will be a "servant of servants", or "lowest of servants" to his brothers. What we see in these verses is prophecy that must have been revealed to Noah by God. Archeology has revealed how debased the Canaanites descended from Canaan would be, practicing prostitution, homosexuality, orgiastic rites, and even child sacrifice[622].

History has further revealed the accuracy of this prophecy in that the four Shemite kings led by Chedorlaomer conquered five Canaanite cities, including Sodom and Gomorrah, making the inhabitants their vassals (Gen 14). (Shem's descendants are known as "Shemites" or "Semites".) Later, the Semite king Solomon "levied forced laborers" from the surviving Canaanites in his land (1Kings 9:20-21). Moses even reinforces the accuracy of this prophecy by adding his editorial comment, "even to this day". Recall that fulfilled biblical prophecy is considered strong support for Divine inspiration, and consequently strong support for the Creation Model.

Noah extends his prophesy to Japheth, predicting that God would "enlarge Japheth", and indeed Japheth had the most descendants, with the Japhethite nations becoming the Persians, Greeks and Romans. We have much evidence, from ancient historical accounts and from archeology, of the ultimate victory of the Romans over the Canaanite nation of Phoenicia and its great maritime capital of Carthage. The Greco-Roman historian, Plutarch, wrote of the wickedness of the Carthaginians in their practice of child sacrifice as part of their worship of their pagan god Baal.[628-629] While the Greeks and Romans also conquered the Semitic nation of Israel, Israel conquered them spiritually. The Hebrew Bible was translated into Greek with the Septuagint. And Jews wrote the entire New Testament in Greek, the "lingua franca" of the Roman Empire. And Christianity spread through the Roman Empire thanks to the *Pax Romana* (Roman Peace).[627]

The most important, and yet the least obvious, point in Noah's prophecy is the reference to "the Lord God of Shem" It is through Shem's descendants that God will reveal His Word, the Bible. And the coming Messiah, the Seed of the Woman (3:15),would be a patrilineal descendant of Shem (Luke 3:36), not of Japheth or Ham.[626]

Genesis 9: 28 – 29 *And Noah lived three hundred and fifty years after the flood. So all the days of Noah were nine hundred and fifty years, and he died.*

According to Dr. Safarti, these verses end the *toledot* of Noah, with the following verse in Chapter 10 beginning the *toledot* of Noah's three sons[632]. Other scholars, like Dr. Henry Morris, consider all three verses to be the ending of the *toledoth* of Shem, Ham and Japheth, comprising a closing "signature", known as a colophon.[8] Support for the Creation Model is manifest with either interpretation, since the account is attributed to be historical narrative either way, as opposed to the contention of skeptics that it is allegorical or mythological.

Noah's lifespan was the third longest in history, exceeded only by Methusaleh (969) and Jared (962). It is interesting to note that after Noah, lifespans of the biblical patriarchs began to decrease, eventually becoming comparable to modern lifespans[678]. The message for Genesis 11 will explore this phenomenon in more detail as a rebuttal to skeptics' claims that the patriarchal lifespans are evidence that the Bible cannot be true history.

Conclusion

By now you should have noticed a recurring theme throughout all these messages. Nothing in the data of "science" contradicts the clear teachings of Scripture up to this point. In this chapter alone, God's Word deals in a very straightforward manner with topics such as: How did we arrive at the population size and genetic make-up that we see today? Why is there fear of man among the wild animals, but other animals can be domesticated? Should mankind be herbivores or omnivores? Why is there so much emphasis on blood in the Bible? What should we think about capital punishment? Could the Flood really have been a worldwide event? Has there been climate change before the industrial era? Why is nakedness associated with shame if we merely evolved from naked apes? What do fulfilled prophecies reveal about the Divine inspiration of Scripture?

My friend, your eternal destiny depends upon your faith in God's Word. However, you are not expected to have a "blind" faith, but rather an informed faith based upon your ability to "give an account for the hope that is within you" (1Pet 3:15). At this point in our series of messages, you are fast approaching the condition of being "without excuse", since you have seen that God's "invisible attributes, His eternal power and divine nature, have been clearly seen, being understood through what has been made ..." (Rom 1:20)

There may be a few issues that remain as stumbling blocks to your accepting God's Word on faith. Maybe one of those stumbling blocks is the age of the earth implied by Scripture being younger than that of the Evolution Model. We will deal with that in the Chapter 11 message. But understand that no number of future messages will answer every question or objection that a skeptic might raise, and you have already seen sufficient evidence supporting the Creation Model as being superior to the Evolution Model. Everyone must ultimately make the choice as to whether to trust the word of God, or the word of fallible, sinful man.

Won't you go ahead and make that choice right now. Jesus warned us in Luke 12 about a man who was preoccupied with expanding his earthly holdings, and did not realize that "This very night your soul is required of you;" If your soul is required of you tonight, are you confident that you will spend eternity with the Lord? The choice you make as to where to place your faith must not be delayed; there is nothing more important than making that decision right now.

Message 10 – Families and Nations

These are the families of the sons of Noah

TEXT: Genesis 10: 1 – 32

Introduction

It is difficult to discuss Genesis Chapter 10, describing the division and geographic dispersion of the clans and family groups descended from Noah, without discussing the events of Chapter 11 which describe *why* the clans and families dispersed. So, here's a spoiler alert: the clans disperse as described in Chapter 10 because God confused their languages in Chapter 11 (shocker!).

Recall the purpose of these messages is not to simply provide a verse-by-verse exposition of Scripture, but to ascertain which theoretical model (Creation or Evolution) provides the best scientific explanation of the available data. As we examine Chapter 10 in this message, you will be relieved to know we will not be examining every verse, which would become quite tedious. Instead, we will be examining the distribution of people groups using the sciences of anthropology and archeology, coupled with what linguistics reveals to us about the evolution of nation names and what reliable recorded history adds to this knowledge.

"Why is this important?", you may ask. When the tools of science collaborate the Genesis narrative, it supports the notion that these passages are *historical records*, and not made-up fables or legends. When we find that the Creation Model is supported as being historical, then the Evolution Model and its "out-of-Africa"[18] human evolution scenario is discredited.

Genesis 10: 1 *Now these are [the records of] the generations of Shem, Ham and Japheth, the sons of Noah; and sons were born to them after the flood.*

Since chapter and verse divisions were not added to Scripture until 1205[653], it is reasonable to assume that this verse is the ending signature of the *toledot* that just ended with the previous verse, since it describes when Noah died. Noah's sons would have the same first-hand knowledge of the events of Chapter 9 as Noah, but on the other hand, Noah would not report on his own death. Following this logic, the following verses will be the *toledot* of Shem according to Gen 11: 1. (For what it's worth, Dr. Sarfati would not agree with my logic, while other scholars would.)

Genesis 10: 2 – 5 *The sons of Japheth were Gomer and Magog and Madai and Javan and Tubal and Meshech and Tiras. And the sons of Gomer were . . . etc.*

So begins what will be a recurring pattern in Genesis 10. First the sons are listed. Second some of the grandsons are listed, to explain the expansion of the nations. Third, the account ends with the settling of the clans into their nations and languages.[634] Another pattern that has already been seen in the earlier genealogies is that first the non-Seed descendants are dispensed with, and then the narrative concentrates on the Seed line leading to the Messiah.

Already Noah's prophecy about "enlarging Japheth" (9:27) is being fulfilled, as Japheth had more sons than either of his brothers. But the enlarging was both in quantity *and* quality, in that the nations were the "coastland peoples" (10:5) around the Mediterranean, Black and Caspian Seas, eventually spreading out to occupy most of Europe, as well as Asia past Persia and India.[639]. Japheth's descendants will also build the great Greek and Roman empires, with their accompanying advances in art, philosophy, architecture, government and technology.

Authenticating the historicity of this passage, consider the additional information about these descendants as revealed by later historical accounts and forensic research[636ff]:

- Gomer: According to the Jewish historian Josephus, he founded "those whom the Greeks now call Galatians [Gauls], but were then called Gomerites". Some of these Gaulish people may have migrated to Britain and become the ancestors of the Welsh.
- Riphath: Chronicles 1: 4-23 copies almost all the names from Genesis 10, showing that later biblical authors took this chapter as historical. One deviation is that in Chronicles this name is listed as "Diphath" in the extant Hebrew text. This is an easy copyist mistake, since both Hebrew names have a very similar first letter.
- Magog: Josephus says that the Greeks called the Magogites "Scythians". They inhabited the western and central steppes of Eurasia and were known for their powerful cavalry.
- Madai: Josephus links Madai to the Medes, a people strongly allied with the Persians and mentioned in many places in the Bible. Indeed, where the Bible refers to the "Medes", the Hebrew word is always "Madai".
- Javan: Josephus writes, "but from Javan, Ionia and all the Grecians are derived." Where the Old Testament refers to Greece, the Hebrew is Javan. The Septuagint transliterated Javan as "Jovan" or "Iovan", and could be the basis for the Roman god, Jove, better known as "Jupiter", the equivalent of the Greek god Zeus.
- Tarshish: This has been connected to Tarsus, later the birthplace of the Apostle Paul. Some scholars think it is more plausible that Tarshish could be Carthage.
- Meshech: The Assyrian name is Mushki, and has been connected to the Meshchera Lowlands of Russia, and may also be connected to the Russian capital, Moscow, old name "Muscovy".

Genesis 10: 6 – 20 *And the sons of Ham were Cush and Mizraim and Put and Canaan. And the sons of Cush were . . . etc.*

The pattern established for the Japhethites is continued with the Hamites. Although Ham had only four sons, many of the Hamite nations are mentioned in this passage, presumably because they became the opponents of the Messianic nation from the time of Moses. We will take a look at some of the more prominent of these to provide further support to the historicity of the narrative as part of the Creation Model.[640ff]

- Cush: Normally thought of as the ancestor of the Ethiopian people, although "Ethiopia" in those times meant all of Africa south of Egypt. By the time of Christ its semantic range was narrowed to mean the land bordering Egypt, called "Nubia" in classical times and now northern Sudan.

- Havilah: This tribe is believed to have settled in what is now Yemen, and in ancient times was a fertile land augmented by irrigation canals, dams and terraced fields.
- Shebah: A grandson of Cush, Sheba was an ancestor of the Sabeans who settled the southern part of the Arabian Peninsula, which was likely the location of the Queen of Sheba who visited Solomon [1Kings 10 and 2 Chron 9).
- Nimrod: Cush fathered Nimrod, who had a reputation as a "mighty hunter before the Lord", which is probably better translated as "in the face of the Lord", implying opposition to God. His reputation as a hunter included the hunting, and enslaving, of men, so that the *Jerusalem Targum* described him as "powerful in wickedness before the Lord". The Bible portrays Nimrod as the first major dictator and empire builder, although he did not father any nations. His empire began with Babel (Babylon) in Shinar, corresponding to modern-day Iraq and portions of Syria, Turkey and Iran. After founding several other cities in Babylonia, he moved to Assyria, founding more cities including Nineveh, the future capital of the Assyrian Empire.
- Mizraim: The name in Hebrew is *mitsrayim*, which is the equivalent of the English, Egypt. The modern **endonym** (the name applied by its own inhabitants) for Egypt is *Misr*.
- Canaan: This is the son of Ham whom Noah cursed. He became the ancestor of a wide variety of Canaanite tribes descended from his eleven sons.
- Sidon: The first-born son of Canaan, Sidon became the eponym of the ancient Phonecian city which is now the third largest city in Lebanon.
- Heth: Heth has been connected with the Hittites, mentioned as a powerful empire several times in the Bible. Since evidence for their existence had not been found, 19th century skeptics claimed they were mythical. However, late in the 19th century the ruins of their huge ancient capital were found in north-central Turkey. The Hittites developed iron smelting and chariots, so were formidable warriors.
- Jebusites: Like most of Canaan's sons, the name of the person is not given, but the descendant people-group is named. These were the inhabitants of Jerusalem before David conquered it and made it his capital (2 Sam 5). The books of Joshua and Judges equate Jebus(ites) with Jerusalem, which is also called Salem in Genesis 14. This chapter has the intriguing story of Salem's priest/king, Melchizedek, meeting and blessing Abraham. Some have proposed that Melchizedek was the patriarch Shem (Noah's son), who would have been still living and probably the oldest man on Earth, but the Bible does not state this.
- Amorites: These occupants of the hill country of Judah may have had some worshipers of the true God, since three Amorite brothers joined with "Abram the Hebrew" in defeating the four eastern kings in Genesis 14, which could explain why God told Abraham he was not yet to have the land of the Canaanites, "for the iniquity of the Amorites is not yet complete" (Gen 15:16). The most famous Amorite was Hammurabi, founder of the original Babylonian Empire, and famous for his 282 harsh laws known as the *Code of Hammurabi*.

Genesis 10: 21 – 24 *And also to Shem, the father of all the children of Eber and the [older] brother of Japheth [the elder], children were born. . . .*

After dispensing with the non-Seed lines of Japheth and Ham, the narrative moves to the Seed line of Shem[650ff]. Since not all of Shem's descendants are in the line to the Messiah, once again the account will deal briefly with them before moving on to Shem's Seed Line in Chapter 11.

The mention of Eber (Shem's great-grandson) is probably a reflection of the fact that of all of Abraham's ancestors, the two that lived the farthest time from the Flood were Shem and Eber, and by the time Abraham was eight years old these would have been his only ancestors still alive – then the two oldest men on Earth as recorded by Scripture.

The ESV and NASV and a number of other translations state that Shem is the older brother of Japheth, but a careful exegesis of other passages shows this cannot be true, and that the KJV and NIV have it correct that "Shem was the brother of Japheth the elder". The inerrancy of the Bible is not at issue here, since the concept of "inerrancy" only applies to the Scriptures in their "original autographs", a phrase that recognizes the obvious reality that mistranslations and copyist errors are bound to occur to some degree over thousands of years, but none of these materially affect the truth of God's Word.

As we have done with the Japhethites and Hamites, we will briefly discuss a few of the prominent non-Seed descendants of Shem, referred to as both "Shemites" and "Semites".

- Elam: Shem's first son was the ancestor of the Elamites, who settled east of Babylon in what was later called Persia, in modern-day Iran. Long before the rise of the Persian Empire, the Elamites figured prominently in biblical history. Chedorlaomer of Elam was the leader of the four kings who subjugated the five kings of Canaan, but the four-king coalition made the huge mistake of capturing Lot from Sodom. Lot's uncle, "Abram the Hebrew" led a tiny army of 318 and utterly demolished the coalition and sent them fleeing past Damascus (Gen 14).
- Asshur: Whenever the English word "Assyria" is used, it is the Hebrew word *ashshur*. These Shemite Assyrians replaced the Hamite Assyrians of Gen 10:11. Assyria later became the powerful empire that overran the northern tribes of Israel.
- Lud: The Bible says little about Shem's fourth son. His name could be connected to Lydia, a district of Asia Minor containing Ephesus, Smyrna, Thyatira and Sardis [Rev 1: 11].
- Aram: Aram is the father of the Aramaeans, or Syrians. The Aramaic language was almost a world language in the ancient world, and even some parts of the Old Testament were first written in Aramaic.[15] One of his four sons, Uz, might have settled the territory in northwestern Mesopotamia described as the homeland of Job [Job 1:1].
- Eber: Eber is descended from Shem's third son, Arpachsad, only mentioned by name, and Eber's father was Shelah, also only mentioned by name, continuing the Seed line from Shem. (As a side note, some Septuagint texts have an extra descendant between Arpachsad and Shelah named Kainan, but this appears to have been a copyist error in later copies of the narrative.) Abraham is called a "Hebrew" in Gen 14. The Hebrew word for a Hebrew person is *ibri* or *ivri*, which seems to be derived from Eber by adding

a "yod" in Hebrew with different vowel points. Eber is also the region of Ur of the Chaldeans, Haran, and Padan-aram (Abraham's original homeland, before God told him to move to the land of Canaan). The narrative moves quickly to Eber's two sons, Peleg and Joktan.

Genesis 10: 25 - 31 *And two sons were born to Eber; the name of the one was Peleg [division], for in his days the earth was divided; and his brother's name was Joktan . . .*

- Peleg: This passage has confused many modern readers who interpret this passage in light of the presumed continental division and subsequent continental drift postulated by the study of plate tectonics. There is really no Scriptural support for such an interpretation for a number of reasons.[651ff]
    - The Hebrew word for earth is *erets*, and in the context of this passage refers to the people of the earth, not Planet Earth.
    - The same Hebrew word is used just a few verses later in 11:1 which states "Now the whole earth [*erets*] had one language . . ." and again in 11:9 where it says, "the Lord confused the language of the whole earth [*erets*]."
    - Before plate tectonics was in vogue, nearly all commentators understood this to be referring to language division, although some claimed it referred to the separation of Peleg's descendants who were sedentary agriculturalists and Joktan's descendants who became the wandering Arab tribes.
    - A seismic event resulting in the division of the earth into continents would have been nearly as destructive as the Flood itself, and would certainly have demanded a more detailed narrative than this. The Creation and Evolution models do not diverge on this point, inasmuch as most creation scientists contend the continental division occurred primarily during the Flood, with only remnant continental drift since; and secular scientists contend the continental division pre-dated human history.
- Joktan and his thirteen sons are dismissed as a non-Seed line and the founders of the Arab tribes. Some of their names have been traced to ancient names of cities and regions associated with Yemen, Saudi Arabia and the Red Sea coast. The fact that thirteen of Joktan's sons are listed, while none of Peleg's are, may indicate that Shem (the presumed author of this *toledot*) was living near Joktan's family.[16]

Genesis 10: 32 *These are the families of the sons of Noah, according to their genealogies, by their nations; and out of these the nations were separated on the earth after the flood.*

The whole section closes by returning to the patriarch of all the post-Flood people, Noah[655]. The 70 nations from Noah's three sons are the progenitors of all other nations, and the gene pool from these six couples provided far more than enough genetic variational potential to account for the wide range of national and tribal characteristics that have surfaced since the Flood. The world's present population of more than seven billion people could have been accomplished easily with an annual growth rate of only a fraction of the current rate, or an

average of 2.5 children per family. The three streams of nations (Japhethites, Hamites and Shemites) listed in Shem's Table of Nations should not be interpreted as three races, however. The concept of race is not found in the Bible and is purely an evolutionary construct with no basis in either Scripture or true science. The Bible speaks only of kinds, whose members are interfertile (i.e., able to reproduce after their *kinds*). Where mankind is concerned, there are nations, tribes, tongues, peoples, and families, but these are not races.[17]
We will examine the origin of the different skin shades and languages in more detail in our study of Genesis 11.

Conclusion

The Creation Model looks to Shem's Table of Nations for a historical narrative explaining the origin of nations and people groups that we have today. Clear connections can be drawn between the patriarchal names and the names of cities, regions and languages that exist today, or are known from written human history. Archaeology, anthropology, linguistics, demographic studies, paleontology and extra-biblical historical accounts all provide substantiating evidence in support of the Creation Model.

The Evolution Model, in contrast, is fractured by numerous competing theories that try to make sense of a skull fragment here, or a footprint there, in defending some researcher's cherished hypothesis of the origins of people groups, or humans in general. Consider the following phrases from separate articles in a single issue of *Scientific American Magazine*[18]:

"controversial new fossils"
"recently discovered species" ... "pushes back the onset of bipedalism to 4MY ago"
"for at least 4 million years, many hominid species shared the planet"
"Out of Africa Again . . . and Again?"
"The Multiregional Evolution of Humans"
"The Recent Africa Genesis of Humans"

The more confusing and complex the Evolution Model gets, the more assured we can be that the Creation Model, especially as laid out in Genesis 10, is the correct model. The biblical narrative has not changed in thousands of years, but the so-called "scientific" explanations change continually. In fact, some of the articles in the aforementioned magazine had sections at the end entitled "Epilogue" where more recent data had changed some of the assertions in the original publication.

How about you? Have you put your faith in the assertions of secular scientists who can't agree among themselves, and have to retract some of their earlier assumptions to accommodate new data? Are you willing to bet your eternal future that we evolved from primitive hominids, who evolved from apes, who evolved from reptiles, amphibians, fish, microbes, and ultimately, from rocks? Oh, and don't forget: the rocks evolved from pure energy which came from nothing!

Isn't it more rational to place your faith in an omniscient Creator who has revealed His divine nature through what has been made [Rom 1:20] and through his divinely inspired Word [2Tim 3:16]? Who loves you so much that he chose to take on human form, endure hardships, torture and execution, to be a suitable sacrifice to take **upon Himself** the penalty we deserve? If you are willing to place your faith in him rather than fake "science", you can be assured your eternity will be spent with Him in eternal life. Placing your faith in anything else, including science, assures that you will be forever separated from Him, which is eternal death.

Will you make the decision right now to choose life over death?

Message 11 – Languages and Genealogies

. . . the Lord scattered them abroad . . .

TEXT: Genesis 11: 1 – 32

Introduction

Genesis 10 and 11 are another example of the literary technique of *recapitulation*[655], similar to what we saw in Genesis 2, which recapitulated the narrative of Genesis 1. Here Genesis 11 is explaining *why* the dispersion of the nations in Genesis 10 happened. The confusion of language may explain why Nimrod left Babel and went to Assyria, and why the Shemite Assyrians were able to overcome the depleted forces of the Hamite Assyrians.

This chapter of Genesis provides us with significant contrasts between the Creation theoretical model and the Evolution Model in describing the origin of the different languages, the *chronogenealogies* as they relate to the age of the earth, and the evidence for cavemen and "primitive" people groups.

Genesis 11: 1 – 2 *Now the whole earth used the same language and the same words. And it came about as they journeyed east, that they found a plain in the land of Shinar and settled there.*

Most biblical scholars believe that the original language was Hebrew, or something close to it. It follows that Adam and Eve spoke this language from the beginning, so it must have been "programmed" into them by God. This is in sharp contrast with the Evolution Model, which supposes language arose from animal grunts in early hominids, but evolutionists are at a loss to explain how the rules of language, called *syntax*, arose.[663] A 2006 study on communication in monkeys found that they lack the necessary brain functions that humans use to perform linguistic computations. Humans have an innate capacity for language, as evidenced by studies on 500 deaf children in Nicaragua who spontaneously developed their own unique sign language, displaying characteristic rules of grammar, and described as the first documented case of the birth of a language.

The plain of Shinar was most certainly the fertile land of Mesopotamia, which would be able to support many people, and where Nimrod built the first post-flood cities.[657] Both secular and biblical scholars are in general agreement that the land between the two great rivers was the "cradle of civilization", but evolutionists struggle to align this fact with their theory that modern humans emerged out of Africa.

Genesis 11: 3 – 4 *And they said to one another, "Come, let us make bricks and burn them thoroughly." And they used bricks for stone, and they used tar for mortar. And they said, "Come, let us build for ourselves a city, and a tower whose top will reach into heaven, and let us make for ourselves a name; lest we be scattered abroad over the face of the whole earth."*

Moses, as the editor of Genesis, points out that kiln-dried bricks joined with asphalt or bitumen were used rather than the usual sun-dried bricks. This construction detail lends a sense of authenticity to the account, since this building method would be strange to the Israelites accustomed to the rocky Promised Land with its abundant stone for building.[657] The tower itself was probably a *ziggurat*, a massive step pyramid that was part of a temple complex.

Building a city and settling down was a direct rebellion against God's command to "fill the earth", and the tower compounded their rebellion. It was to "reach into heaven", probably intended for astrological worship of the heavenly bodies, and its height might have been provision for escape from another flood if God intended to break His covenant promise. Furthermore, their intention to "make for ourselves a name" indicates a form of sinful humanistic pride. According to the Jewish historian, Josephus, it was Nimrod who led them "to such an affront and contempt of God."

Not surprisingly, God will not let this rebellion persist.

Genesis 11: 5 – 8

This passage uses an *anthropomorphism*[660], depicting God in a human-like way "coming down", seeing the rebellious acts, and deciding to confuse their languages, with the result that the various clans and tribes dispersed from the region and "stopped building the city".

Genesis 11: 9 *Therefore its name was called Babel [Babylon], because there the Lord confused the language of the whole earth; and from there the Lord scattered them abroad over the face of the whole earth.*

It is time to pause and reflect on this momentous event. It is the fourth of the "big C's" of history, "Confusion", which was preceded by the first three: (1) Creation, (2) Corruption / Curse, and (3) Catastrophe. If the biblical account is true, then the Creation Model should find support, to the detriment of the Evolution Model, in the following categories:

1. **Languages –** The Babel account would predict that languages, having been confused by God himself, should be able to be grouped today into classifications that bear little resemblance to each other. On the other hand, if human language evolved slowly from animal grunts[667], the Evolution Model would predict that all modern languages should be able to be traced back to the same proto-language in at least some aspects.

Today there are estimated to be 6,000 to 7,000 languages, with many variations called dialects, some of which developed to be so different that they were no longer intelligible to the original speakers and became new languages[664]. Linguists have been able to trace many of these thousands of languages back to fewer ancestral languages, but there is a limit – a *single* ancestral common language of *all* languages is out of reach![664]

The thousands of different languages fall into a relatively small number of language *families*. French, Spanish, Portuguese, Italian and Romanian are called the *Romance* languages because they were derived from Latin, the language of ancient Rome. The *Germanic* languages include English and are derived from a Proto-Germanic. The *Slavonic* languages include Russian. There are deeper similarities among all these, as well as Sanskrit and the Indian languages, so that they are further grouped into the *Indo-European* family, all of which are thought to descend from a Proto-Indo-European ancestor language.

However, some European languages, such as Hungarian, are disconnected from all of these and so are grouped into the *Uralic* language family. The *Semitic* languages, of which Hebrew is a member, are different again. Hebrew is similar to Arabic and Aramaic, but they are now unintelligible to each other, but clearly derived from a common ancestral language. This explains why the Judean leaders in King Hezekiah's time asked the Assyrian captain to speak in Aramaic, rather than Hebrew, so the Jewish people would not understand (2Kings 18:26). The similarities among languages of a given family show how thousands of languages could have arisen from just a few ancestral languages, with the original languages being totally disconnected (confused) from each other.

The Bible does not specify how many different languages there were initially, but from Shem's table of nations in Genesis 10, we can make a reasonable guess of 70 (26 from Shem, 30 from Ham and 14 from Japheth). After the initial scattering, some people groups would have mixed and learned at least some portions of another group's language due to conquests, political alliances, etc., producing a hodge-podge of languages that would be difficult to define categorically. For example, English has borrowed words from other languages, created new words from Latin or Greek roots (especially in science), and simply invented new words out of thin air. (If you don't believe me, google it!)

The Evolution Model's explanation of language finds no supporting evidence for a single ancestral language.[667] In fact, the evidence shows just the opposite. There is no hint of build-up from simpler language. Ancient languages were actually extremely complex with many different inflections. Modern descendants of these languages have greatly reduced the number of inflections, i.e., the trend is from complex to simpler, the opposite of evolution. English has almost completely lost inflections, retaining just a few like the possessive **–'s**. Also, English has lost 65-85% of the Old English vocabulary, and a similar trend is seen in the lost vocabulary of the Romance languages from the original Latin.

2. **Races** – If Babel resulted into the separation of people groups, then each group would contain only a portion of the total human gene pool. Secular scientists agree that this isolation of small people groups will help to fix certain characteristics in each isolated population. Natural selection and sexual selection would also act to "fine tune" the results.[668] However, the Evolution Model does not offer an explanation of *how* this separation and isolation were able to persist (except in geographically isolated populations like islanders or those separated by mountain ranges or deserts), since evolutionists do not envision language barriers as a causative agent.

As the Hamite tribes dispersed to Africa, increasing exposure to harmful ultraviolet (UV) rays would favor those individuals with more of the pigment *melanin* in their skin, since they would be more protected from skin cancer, tropical diseases and reproductive impairment due to diminished levels of the essential B vitamin folate in their blood.[19] Hence natural selection and sexual selection would favor dark skin in these tribes and families.

On the other hand, Japhethites who migrated to the higher latitudes would need lighter skin, since the sunscreen effect of melanin would prevent UVB radiation from penetrating the epidermis in order to stimulate the production of Vitamin D. This would result in calcium deficiency, with negative effects on skeletal development and the immune system[19]. Again, natural selection and sexual selection would result in lighter skin in the European and Scandinavian countries. A deviation from this tendency toward lighter skin is seen in the Inuit people of Alaska and northern Canada, whose skin is darker than would be expected in a region of such low solar radiation. Apparently, their diet of fish and marine mammals provides them with sufficient Vitamin D to offset the inability to synthesize Vitamin D in their skin.

Medium brown or olive is the most common skin shade throughout the middle latitudes. These people migrated across Asia, ultimately crossing the Bering Strait into the Americas. By this time, they had lost the genetic information for very dark skin, so even those in equatorial South America are still quite medium-complexioned[671].

Besides skin color, other traits that would be selected in isolated population groups include eye color, eye shape, hair color, hair texture and blood group. Since any human can reproduce sexually with any other human of the opposite sex, we are all one species, and according to Acts 17:26, all one blood. Therefore, the differences we see among various people groups are not indicative of different races at all. There is only one race – the human race.

For at least 100 years, on the other hand, the Evolution Model proclaimed that humans are divided into five races, and that the Caucasian race was the most evolved, the Negro least evolved. This racist view has been disproven by modern genetics; a fact now being acknowledged by evolutionist publications like *Scientific American Magazine*:[19]

> "Early Western scientists used skin color improperly to delineate human races, but the beauty of science is that it can and does correct itself. . . . We look ahead to the day when the vestiges of old scientific mistakes will be erased and replaced by a better understanding of human origins and diversity."

To that I say, "AMEN". (But don't hold your breath until evolutionists adopt this philosophy.)

3. **Cavemen –** According to the Creation Model, the drastic climate change after the Flood would have resulted in the Ice Age that persisted for 500-700 years. Warm oceans from the break-up of the "fountains of the great deep" would evaporate enormous amounts of water vapor, which would then condense and fall as snow on the upper latitude continents. These, in turn, would experience cool summers due to suspended aerosols from multitudes of active volcanoes. The dispersing clans and tribes from Babel would leave behind their collective knowledge of building construction, metal smelting and tool making, taking with them only a few things that would soon deteriorate and become unusable.

These dispersing people groups would find themselves in unfamiliar environments, already populated by the descendants of the Ark animals that had obeyed God's command to fill the earth. They would have to become hunter-gatherers, and what better shelter for the time-being than caves? The only materials available to them for fashioning tools, knives and weapons were rocks, bone and wood. Igneous stones could be formed into hammers, and flint could be flaked to make sharp knives, spears and arrows. Human ingenuity would enable them to hunt or trap large animals for food, fur and hides, and their knowledge of fire-making would enable them to fend off wild animals, cook food and warm their cave homes. Eventually they would find a place to settle down, construct buildings, plant crops and divide labors according to talents and skills. Ultimately elaborate cities would emerge, and unsurprisingly, pyramids and ziggurats would begin to crop up wherever they went. Caves would still be found useful for burial of the dead, even up to the modern historical era.

The Evolution Model, on the other hand, depicts ancient human cave dwellers as primitive brutes who took thousands of years just to improve on the design of a stone axe. Consequently, evolutionists are continually being surprised by new findings that show:

a) Ancient cave paintings of animals are very sophisticated, with astonishingly accurate illustrations of animal motions. A research team found that cave paintings had a lower error rate in depicting anatomy than many modern era artworks, including those of Leonardo da Vinci[674].
b) Neanderthals, once thought to be barely evolved apes, have been found to have practiced burial rituals, made jewelry, concocted a precursor to aspirin from plants, consumed the antibiotic-producing mold *Penicillium*, made advanced bone and stone tools, built huts and hearths, and invented a "super glue" for attaching spear tips. Depicted for decades as walking with a stooped, ape-like posture, more recent research has shown "Neanderthal posture and movement would have been the same as ours"[20].
c) Ancient people groups developed advanced seafaring skills. Though no remnants of their boats remain, they clearly could traverse large areas of open ocean requiring navigational ability.
d) Ancient structures from Stonehenge to Peru show advanced skills in construction, stone working, engineering and astronomy that defy explanation to this day.

Clearly the Creation Model's description of the dispersal from Babel provides the superior explanation for the findings of archeologists, paleontologists, anthropologists and linguists as compared to the Evolution Model.

Genesis 11: 10 – 11 *These are the records of the generations of Shem. Shem was one hundred years old, and became the father of Arpachshad two years after the flood; and Shem lived 500 years after he became the father of Arpachshad, and he had other sons and daughters.*

A new tablet begins with Gen 11:11, and will close with 11:17. Since Shem was 100 years old two years after the flood, he must have been born when Noah was 502. That means that the son born when Noah was 500 (Gen 5: 32) must have been Japheth, since Ham was called the youngest in Gen 9: 24.

Genesis 11: 12 – 26

These verses follow a pattern similar to what we saw in the *chronogenealogies* of Gen 5:

When **A** had lived **x** years, he fathered **B**. And **A** lived after he fathered **B**

y years, and had other sons and daughters.

One difference in these chronogenealogies compared to Chapter 5 is that the total number of years of **A** is not given in Chapter 11, but that is a minor difference, since simple arithmetic will allow one to arrive at the approximate age at death. For example, we can deduce that Shem must have lived 600 or 601 years, since the number of years is rounded to the nearest whole number. Note that this would mean that during Abram's (Abraham's) lifetime, Shem was still living! In fact, the Targums of Jerusalem and Jonathan claim that after the Babel dispersion, Shem settled in Jerusalem, became its king, and took the Jebusite name *Melchizedek*[678], presumably the same priest-king (and archetype of Christ) to whom Abram gave a tenth of his spoils of battle in Genesis 14: 18 – 20.

With Genesis Chapters 5 and 11 we have an unbroken chronology of the history of mankind from Adam thru Abraham. Both creationist and secular scholars have a good understanding of the historical setting for Abraham, so by adding up the chronogenealogies we can arrive at a close approximation of the age of the earth. Two profound revelations emerge from a study of these verses that require serious scrutiny as they relate to support for either the Creation Model or the Evolution Model:

1. Lifespans for the patriarchs diminish rapidly following the Flood, declining from nearly 1,000 years in the antediluvian period, to essentially modern lifespans of 45 years by the time of Christ. (Lifespans have increased considerably in the last two centuries due to improvements in nutrition, hygiene and medical arts.)

Skeptics have tried to claim that the ages of the post-Flood patriarchs were adjusted by scribes to compensate for the "obviously inflated" ages of the pre-Flood generations, in an attempt to lend greater credibility to the biblical account. There is no evidence for such a claim, other than the assumptions inherent in the Evolution Model. However, modern scientific research provides several logical reasons why lifespans *would* decrease after the Flood:

a) Decay of Earth's magnetic field – Our planet has a protective magnetic field (to be discussed more later) which tends to divert harmful cosmic radiation around the earth, much like the bow wave of a boat. This field has been measured by scientists for several hundred years, and it is now well known that the field strength has been decaying exponentially[135, 686]. This decay of our magnetic "shield" means more and more cosmic radiation can reach Earth's surface, causing damage to cellular DNA and more and more genetic mutations. As these mutations accumulate with each generation, the resulting genetic damage will result in shortened lifespans.

b) Noah's advanced age at the conception of his surviving sons[687] – It has long been known that children born to older mothers have a higher risk of developing genetic disorders, and it is reasonable to assume Mrs. Noah's age was comparable to Noah's.
More recently, research has shown that aged fathers are also a major source of genetic disorders, so Shem and all his descendants had much lower lifespans than the pre-Flood patriarchs.

So modern research supports the biblical account and the Creation Model, giving logical explanations as to why lifespans would decrease following the Flood. Secular scientists, with their Evolution Model, would predict drastically shorter lifespans in the pre-scientific era, with longer lifespans only arising in modern history with the advancement of knowledge.

2. Adding up the years given in the chronogenealogies of Genesis, coupled with the king lists in the remainder of the Old Testament, yield an age for the earth of 6,000-7,000 years. Dr. Sarfati's calculation gives a date of Creation as **4178 ± 50** BC, yielding a total age (as of 2021) of roughly **6,200** years. Probably the most famous calculation of the earth's age was done by Archbishop James Ussher, whose estimate was about 170 years younger. Other scholars have offered dates for Creation ranging from nearly 7,000BC to 3,616BC, but no one can make a *biblical* case for the earth being any older than 10,000 years.

The idea of evolution over billions of years cannot tolerate a short timescale of thousands of years. This is probably the most critical difference between the Evolution and Creation models, because without millions or billions of years, the Evolution Model totally collapses**.** One would think that with the tools that science has at its disposal today, it should be a simple task to ascertain the "true" age of the earth.

Surprisingly, it is not that simple to determine the age of something. What is needed is something like a geological "hourglass" for which:

a. the initial conditions are known,
b. the rate of change is constant over time, and
c. the system is closed (i.e., matter or energy cannot enter or leave the system).

Unfortunately, no such system exists in the real world, so scientist must make assumptions and adjustments to arrive at an estimate of age, which often means we must settle for a range between a minimum and maximum. Some candidates for such an "hourglass" are:

1) The rate of decay in the earth's magnetic field – The current in the earth that produces this field has been documented and measured to have a half-life of 1,600 years. If we calculate back a mere 30,000 years, the current would have been strong enough to melt the earth! Clearly this is way more than a maximum possible age for the earth.[21]
2) The rate at which salt accumulates in the oceans – Salt is entering the ocean (due to erosion of the crust) faster than it is leaving. Calculations show that a maximum age for the oceans is 62 million years, <u>assuming there was no salt to begin with</u>. This maximum age is way too small to support the Evolution Model.[135]
3) The rate of erosion from continents – Each year about 20 billion tons of dirt and rock erode from the continents and are deposited by rivers and streams onto the ocean floor.[22] At this rate, the entire North American continent would have eroded down to sea level in less than 10 million years.[23] To illustrate the absurdity of the Evolution

Model's timeframe, consider that there are exposed dinosaur fossils on the Colorado Plateau allegedly 65 million years old, at an elevation of a mile above sea level.

4) The rate of lunar recession – The moon and Earth exert tidal forces on each other. This causes the earth's rotation to slow, and according to the principle of Conservation of Angular Momentum, the moon moves away from the earth at the rate of about 1-1/2 inches per year. This rate in nonlinear, being greater in the past, and calculations have shown that the moon would have been touching the earth less than 1-1/2 billion years ago, far less than its assumed secular age of 4.5 billion years. Of course, the Creation Model contends the moon was created approximately where it is today – or possibly 1,000 feet closer - 6,000 years ago.
5) Radiometric dating – It will surprise many to learn that the tools used by scientists to "date" rock ages to millions, or even billions, of years actually show the opposite when the data is properly interpreted. Carbon-14 dating can only be used to date remains of once-living artifacts, and then only if they are younger than 100,000 years (the detection limit for carbon-14). However, no carbon-based artifact has ever been found this old, because every sample ever tested still contains measurable carbon-14; including coal, fossil shells and even diamonds (assumed by secular scientists to be a billion years old or more). Other types of radiometric dating (e.g., uranium-lead, potassium-argon, etc.) fail on the assumptions of a constant rate of change, a closed system, and/or initial boundary conditions.

A more complete discussion of the earth-age controversy is warranted, but we will defer it to the Epilogue, the next and final message. That discussion may go too far "into the weeds" for some who may not recall much of their nuclear chemistry or physics. For now, we will summarize the findings of science with the following statistics compiled by Dr. Henry Morris:

In analyzing 67 different methods for estimating Earth's maximum possible age, 23 yielded ages less than 10,000 years, 10 gave ages between 10,000 and 100,000 years, 11 between 100,000 and 1 million years, and 23 between 1 million and 500 million years[24]. None of these supports anything close to the amount of time needed for the Evolution Model to be even remotely plausible. Only the 68th method, radiometric dating, could arrive at the necessary billions of years, but as we shall see in the Epilogue, this is only if one ignores the discrepant data and the faulty assumptions associated with that method.

Genesis 11: 27 – 32

These verses close the *toledot* of Terah and begin the lengthy tablet of Abraham, which extends all the way to Gen 25. It seems that the *toledot* statements begin at that point to introduce the tablet that follows, rather than ending one preceding it (as Dr. Sarfati contends is true of all the *toledots*).

Since the Evolution Model does not concern itself much with the remaining Genesis narrative, our comparison of the two theoretical models ends here.

Conclusion

Only in the mind of an evolutionist would a 6,000+ year-old Earth be considered "young", but in comparison with the Evolution Model, the Creation Model yields what many would call a "young earth". However, creationist ministries like Answers in Genesis and Creation Ministries International do not tout themselves as "young earth creationists" (YEC's), but rather claim only to be *biblical* creationists. In defending the authority of the Bible, they sadly must devote a disproportionate amount of time to debating "old-earthers". Please do not misunderstand this statement, because believing in a young earth is not a salvation issue. Many sincere Christians believe that the Bible can be interpreted to accommodate millions of years, and even biological evolution, and that's fine. I'm not concerned with their salvation; I'm concerned with yours.

If you have been skeptical about the claims of Genesis 1 – 11, or maybe even just a little bit uncomfortable, my prayer is that this series of messages has helped you see that there is nothing "unscientific" about the Creation Model. Dr. Arno Penzias, Nobel laureate and co-discoverer of the cosmic microwave background radiation (claimed by evolutionists to be the "echo of the big bang") has said, "that the creation of the universe is supported by all the observable data astronomy has produced so far."[25] For over 160 years, most secular scientists have declared allegiance to the Evolution Model, and many have tried to discredit the Creation Model, so it is not surprising that most people have trouble with Genesis 1 – 11. It's a dirty little secret among the evolutionists that a number of scientists from all over the world have signed a statement critical of the big bang theory (cosmologystatement.org), and over 1,000 science Ph.D's have signed "A Scientific Dissent from Darwinism" despite a warning on the web page that "expressing dissent from Darwinism can generate controversy and be unsafe, especially for those who haven't earned tenure" (dissentfromdarwin.org).

With apologies to Dr. Penzias, I paraphrase his statement as, "The Creation Model is supported by all the observable data scientific research has produced so far."

Here's the bottom line: science has not disproven the Bible. The apostle Paul told us that the unbeliever is without excuse in Rom 1:20, and in 1Tim 6:20 that we are to avoid "worldly and empty chatter and the opposing arguments of what is falsely called knowledge" [literally "pseudo-science" in the Greek]. In Paul's day the pseudo-science took the form of Epicureanism (based on atheistic evolutionism) or Stoicism (based on pantheistic evolutionism), which later "evolved" as Gnosticism, then neo-Platonism. In other parts of the world, it had the form of Taoism, Hinduism, Confucianism or Buddhism, all based on some form of pantheistic evolution and an infinitely old cosmos. In recent times it assumed the form of Darwinism, though men are now returning again to various forms of eastern religion and their systems of pantheistic evolution, still rejecting Christ as Creator and Savior.[26]

If you have never claimed Jesus Christ as your Creator and Savior, every excuse has been taken from you. Now is the time to submit to Him as Lord and master of your life. Please pray this prayer right now:

"Lord, I admit that I am a hopeless sinner. I believe you are who your Word says you are, and that you came to Earth to live among us and be the perfect sacrifice for our sins. I ask you to come into my heart and help me to be the person you want me to be. Amen."

Epilogue

And do not be conformed to this world, but be transformed by the renewing of your mind . . . [Romans 12:2]

Introduction

Some have said we are now in a post-Christian era, where materialism, humanism and secularism are the doctrines of the predominant worldview. Scientists have been portrayed as the "high priests" of this new religion, but only those with particular opinions are approved by the ruling elites – those who possess the power in politics, government, academia, media and corporations. We have seen a "cancel culture" emerge, intent on silencing any dissenters from the approved dogma on scientific issues such as climate change, corona virus policy and medical ethics. But nowhere is the battle more intense than in the scientific debate over creation/evolution. In his book, *Slaughter of the Dissidents*, Dr. Jerry Bergman has documented hundreds of cases of overt discrimination and recriminations against creationist scientists, authors and academics, resulting in loss of tenure, termination of employment, blacklisting from publishing and libelous attacks on their reputations.

No human – not even the scientist – has a hold on Ultimate Truth. Science especially is always uncertain, capable of falsification and subject to alternate explanations for every observed phenomenon. Science progresses by advancing theories which are later modified or abandoned in favor of better explanations. Aristotle was supplanted by Ptolemy, who in turn yielded to the Copernican model reinforced by Galileo, Brahe, Kepler and Newton. Much later Hubble upended much of their theories, and Einstein much more so with his theories of relativity. Even Einstein was perplexed by the findings in quantum physics by Heisenberg and others. People who choose to make science their religion will find that their "gods" are hopelessly capricious.

In this series of messages, the Evolution Model has been shown to be a total failure in explaining the data observed in operational science. The only alternative – the Creation Model – has been shown to be a vastly superior explanatory tool. Are there still unresolved questions? Absolutely! No one (human) can have all the answers about everything.

In this epilogue we will attempt to tie up a few loose ends, and drive home some points made previously. In so doing, the intention is that your faith will grow more informed and more confident in our omniscient, eternal and omnipotent Creator. **His fingerprints are all over His creation**.

Evidence for the Fine Tuning of the Universe[27]

- Forty different elements must be able to share or trade electrons to bond together to produce molecules and compounds. If the electromagnetic force were any stronger, atoms would hang onto their electrons too tightly, but if any weaker, atoms would not hang onto their electrons at all. In addition, the ratio of proton mass to electron mass must be similarly fine-tuned.

- If the strong nuclear force were only 2% weaker, protons would not stick together to form the nucleus of the atom and we would have only hydrogen in the universe. If only 0.3% stronger, there would be only the heavier elements with no possibility for life.
- If the neutron was only 0.1% more massive, there would be too few of them to form the nucleus of the heavier elements. If it was only 0.1% less massive, protons would decay so rapidly into neutrons that the universe would collapse into neutron stars or black holes.
- The number of electrons in the universe must equal the number of protons to one part in 10^{37}. This would be the equivalent of finding a particular dime in a pile of dimes covering an area a billion times that of North America, to a height of 239,00 miles (the average distance to the moon).
- The rate at which the universe is expanding must be within one part in 10^{55} of what it is.
- The ratio of the electromagnetic force to the gravitational force must be precisely what it is to within one part in 10^{40}.
- The ratio of energy levels between carbon-12 to oxygen-16 (the most abundant isotopes of these elements) must be what it is or there would be insufficient amounts of both elements to support life.
- The polarity of the water molecule must be what it is for all three forms (solid, liquid and gas) to coexist on the planet and for life chemistry to function.

Evidence for Design in Specified Complexity of Systems

"Complexity" by itself does not necessarily imply design. For example, a snowflake may seem complex under a microscope, but its intricate crystal arrangement is merely a product of hydrogen bonding among water molecules, which could have just as well arranged themselves in innumerable other arrangements. "Specified complexity" implies a purpose-oriented design, every detail of which is critical to the ultimate purpose of the system, and therefore can only be achieved by an intelligence directing the process.

- DNA, according to Microsoft founder Bill Gates, is the most complex code in the universe. Nearly every cell in the body contains a copy of the 3 billion nucleotides that comprise the human genome. Not only does the code control how the organism develops from egg or seed, it also controls the day-to-day functions of the mature adult form. We now know that the code is written so that it can be read forward and backwards, and that sections of code can be "cut and spliced" as needed to initiate certain functions. It is 3-dimensional in its spooled arrangement around histones, and it can find and repair its own errors, not to mention direct its own replication. No software engineer can begin to fathom how to emulate this.
- The nucleotides in DNA group themselves into triplets called codons, which in turn specify the amino acids that ultimately sequence themselves to form into proteins. A typical gene within DNA has about 1,000 base-pairs, so the possible number of variations in the coding for a protein is around 10^{602}. This is an unimaginably huge number, given that

the total number of atoms in the universe is "only" 10^{80}. Research has shown that only a tiny fraction of these possible arrangements could yield a functional protein, so mathematics and probability theory rule out the possibility of random arrangements of amino acids self-assembling into useful proteins, thereby disproving one of the fundamental tenets of evolution.

- Even if a functional protein is arrived at somehow, it is useless until it is folded into the proper 3-dimensional shape. The cellular machinery that does this is not understood at all yet, but researchers are beginning to unravel how a *given* amino acid sequence will fold. Google's AI (artificial intelligence) subsidiary, DeepMind, announced at the end of 2020 that its latest AlphaFold software can accurately predict the folding of a protein based solely on its amino acid sequence with 92.4% accuracy[28]. While it is certainly an admirable achievement that scores of scientists armed with the most sophisticated computers and algorithms can predict the folding of a known functional sequence, it pales in comparison to the Designer of the program that *directs* non-living molecules to self-assemble into the building blocks of life.
- Earth's environment and its biosphere are too exquisitely engineered to be the result of chance or accident. Our moon is close enough and large enough to protect the earth from asteroids, comets and meteorites. The moon's gravitational pull is just right for generating cleansing tides that renew the estuaries and littoral zones twice daily, yet not so strong that the tides cause massive erosion to coastlines. Earth's atmosphere has just the right mixture of gases to fuel cellular respiration and photosynthesis, yet without oxidizing and burning up life forms. Earth's mass is just right for holding its atmosphere, yet not so large that it produces a crushing atmospheric pressure like that of Venus. Earth's distance from the sun is just right for allowing oceans of liquid water to limit vast temperature swings, while still allowing ice and vapor states to sustain the water cycle. The planet's 23- ½ ° tilt of its rotational axis allows for seasons in the mid and upper latitudes, resulting in favorable temperatures to sustain diverse life forms. Hundreds of other examples can be cited[29].

Evidence for Simultaneous Creation of Interacting Systems

The classic "chicken and egg" dilemma shows up all over the creation, requiring that two or more complex systems would have had to evolve *simultaneously* to be of any use[232ff].

- DNA's code requires many different decoding machines to read it. However, the instructions to build this decoding machinery are themselves stored on the DNA.
- Cellular processes require energy, supplied by a molecule called ATP. ATP is produced by the molecular machine *ATP synthase*, but this machine cannot be produced without instructions in the DNA, read by decoding machines powered by (you guessed it) ATP; a three-way egg-chicken-egg dilemma!
- A similar situation exists with the machines that DNA needs to copy itself. These copying machines cannot be passed on without the copying machines already being present.

- Plants need energy to power their cellular respiration, a chemical process with many intricate parts. This energy is supplied by plant sugars. But the plant must produce these sugars by photosynthesis, another chemical process with many different moving parts. Both processes had to appear simultaneously, and begin operating immediately, for the plant to live.
- Placental mammals (like us humans) give birth to live young. In giving birth, several of the mother's arteries that served the placenta are severed. The mother would quickly bleed to death were it not for an ingenious process that closes off the arteries like purse strings. What an amazing stroke of luck for the evolutionists that this feature evolved just in time for the first placental mammal to survive![30]

Evidence for a Young Earth; But What About Radiometric Dating?!

In Message 11 we discussed the various "geological hourglasses" that could be used to date the age of the earth, and we found that of 68 methods examined, only one – radiometric dating – could yield anywhere near the billions of years required for the Evolution Model to work, even allowing the most generous assumptions for an old Earth.

One radiometric method, however, using the carbon-14 isotope, actually proves a young *biosphere*, but it can only be used on artifacts that were once living. Since its methodology differs somewhat from the other radiometric methods used to date rocks, we will discuss it separately from the others after a little bit of "nuclear physics 101":

<u>Background Information</u>

All atoms are composed of a nucleus containing one or more positively-charged protons, and some number of neutrons (except for the simplest form of hydrogen). The number of protons determines the *atomic number*, and this number uniquely determines the identity of the element. For example, atomic number 1 is hydrogen, 2 is helium, 6 is carbon, 92 is uranium.

Neutrons have neutral electric charge, but are important for helping to hold the nucleus together, and the neutron has a mass equal to the mass of a proton. Adding up the number of protons and neutrons in the nucleus gives us the *mass number* of the atom, and this number is used to identify the *isotope* of the element. For example, hydrogen-1 has one proton and zero neutrons; hydrogen-2 (also called *deuterium*) has 1 proton and 1 neutron. Hydrogen-3 (also called *tritium*) has 1 proton and 2 neutrons. Carbon-14 has 6 protons and 8 neutrons, while carbon-12 (the most common form of carbon) has 6 and 6. Uranium-235 has 92 protons and 143 neutrons, while uranium-238 has three more neutrons (146).

Most atoms have just the right number of neutrons relative to protons to have a stable isotope. Having more or fewer neutrons will make the nucleus unstable, hence the isotope is considered unstable or *radioactive*. Some atoms do not have any stable isotope; in other words, *all* of its isotopes are unstable. Uranium is probably the best known unstable, or radioactive, element.

An unstable nucleus is always seeking a more stable state. It will spit a particle out of its nucleus in an effort to arrive at a stable isotope. It may spit out an *alpha particle* (symbol α) consisting of 2 protons and 2 neutrons. Note that this will reduce the atomic number by 2, so the atom now has a new identity on the Periodic Table of the Elements. Also, the mass number will decrease by 4. For example, uranium-238 will become thorium-234. Alternatively, the nucleus can spit out a *beta particle* (symbol β), which is identical to a negatively-charged electron, but instead of coming from the electron cloud surrounding the nucleus (remember your chemistry!), it comes out of one of the neutrons in the nucleus. But now that neutron is no longer electrically neutral, so it can't be a neutron anymore. Since the mass of the electron (or beta particle) is negligible compared to either a proton or neutron, the mass number of the atom will not change, but the neutron has changed to a positively-charged proton, so the atomic number goes *up* by 1. For example, thorium-234 (atomic number 90) will become protactinium-234 (atomic number 91). Still unstable, this atom will again undergo beta decay, taking the atom's identity back to uranium, but a different isotope: uranium-234. This *decay chain* for uranium-238 has a total of 8 alpha decay steps and 6 beta decay steps before finally reaching a stable (ground) state as lead-206. At every step in the decay series, we say that a *parent isotope* has decayed into a *daughter isotope*. Generally, we refer to the initial isotope as the parent, and the final stable isotope as the daughter.

If you are not already confused, we will add another wrinkle. There is no way of knowing when a particular unstable atom will undergo radioactive decay; it may be in the next millisecond, or in a billion years. However, in a rock sample containing let's say a trillion atoms of uranium-238, we know from experimentation and calculations how long *statistically* it will take for *half* of the unstable atoms to decay to the next step in the chain. We call this statistical time period the *half-life* of that isotope.

For example, in 4.5 billion years, half of the atoms in a sample of uranium 238 will decay into thorium 234. Curiously, the half-life of thorium 234 is only 24.5 days. Other half-lives in the 16 steps of decay range from hundreds of thousands, to tens of thousands to thousands of years, down to days, minutes and fractions of a second. Since the first decay step is billions of years, the remaining steps don't change the total decay time to get to lead very much, so it is correct to round the time for half of the uranium-238 to decay into lead-206 to simply 4.5 billion years.

For a simplistic example, if we find a rock sample containing 3 grams of uranium-238 and 3 grams of lead-206, it would seem that one half-life, or 4.5 billion years, have gone by since the rock first formed. Actual field measurements and calculations are not that simple, but the calculations of age still rest upon the same ***assumptions*** if the method is to be able to date a rock:

1. The initial amount of parent (uranium-238) is known (here assumed to be 6 grams).
2. The rate of radioactive decay in all (16) steps has not changed over 4.5 billion years.
3. No substances have entered / left the rock sample in 4.5 billion years (closed system).
4. None of the daughter isotopes were present in the rock to begin with, so therefore:
   All the daughter isotope (lead-206) is only from decay of parent (uranium-238).

In addition to the uranium-lead decay series, other decay series have been used to attempt to date rocks: potassium-argon, rubidium-strontium, lead-lead, thorium-lead, samarium-neodymium etc., but they all depend on the assumptions listed above. Even a casual observer can see these assumptions are on shaky ground.

Problems with Radiometric Dating

1. When radiometric dating is used on rocks *of known age*, the calculations yield vastly inflated ages[31]:
   a. Rocks formed in 1065 at Sunset Crater, AZ were dated at 200,000+ years.
   b. Rocks formed in the 20th century at Mt. Nguarhoe in New Zealand dated at 275,000 years to 3.9 billion years[33].
   c. Basalt rock formed in 1801 at Hualalai, HI was dated at up to 2.2 million years
   d. Basalt from a 1972 eruption at Mt. Etna, Sicily dated at up to 350,000 years.
   e. Rocks formed in the 1980 eruption of Mt. St. Helens dated to 2.8 million years.

2. Wildly different ages are calculated when using different methods on the *same rock*[33]. For example, at Mt. Nguarhoe the following dates were obtained:
   a. Using rubidium-strontium method: 133 million years
   b. Using potassium-argon: 270,000 to 3.5 million years
   c. Using lead-lead: 3.9 billion years
   d. Using samarium-neodymium: nearly 200 million years

3. Dating schemes yield results that are obviously in conflict with common sense. For example, wood buried in volcanic basalt was dated at 45,000 years by carbon-14 dating, while the rock surrounding it was dated to 44 billion years using potassium-argon radiometric dating. Basalts in the Grand Staircase's Uinkaret Plateau were dated older than the lava flows *beneath* them by hundreds of millions of years.[31]

4. Rocks are demonstrably not closed systems (assumption #3):
   a. Some of the daughter isotopes are gases (e.g., radon, argon) which can freely move into and out of rock formations.
   b. Many of the isotopes are soluble in water (e.g., uranium salts) and can move in and out of rock formations. This also means that there is no way of knowing the initial amount of the parent isotope (assumption #1)

5. Recently formed volcanic basalts are typically found to already contain the daughter isotope (e.g., argon) at the time they are formed (assumption #4).

6. Strong evidence exists that decay rates were faster in the past (assumption #2). For example, helium atoms (essentially the same as alpha particles) leak out of zircon crystals containing uranium. But experimental data shows that the rate of helium leakage dates the crystals to thousands of years, while decay data indicate millions or billions of years

of decay at today's rate as applied to the assumed half-lives.[32] Accelerated nuclear decay in the past may have been caused by mechanisms related to the initiation of the Flood, or perhaps radiation storms from solar flares or nearby supernovae. Recent research has shown that decay rates can accelerate from the current accepted values by a factor of 10^9 – that's a *billion* times faster.[34]

Carbon-14 Dating

Dating of once-living or organic artifacts using Carbon-14 is a different physical process involving both nuclear and organic chemistry, and so merits its own discussion.

All living organisms exchange carbon with their environment. Plants take in carbon in the molecular form of carbon dioxide (CO_2), and also sequester carbon in the form of carbohydrates. Animals consume this sequestered carbon when they eat plant tissue (or other animals), and then return it to the environment in cellular respiration and decomposition reactions. The element carbon occurs in three isotopes: carbon-12 (98.93%), carbon-13 (1.07%) and carbon-14[35]. In a sample of one trillion carbon atoms, only one will be carbon-14. There is no difference in the chemical properties of the three carbon isotopes, so living systems will use carbon-14 in the same way they use carbon-12. However, carbon-14 has an unstable nucleus and will undergo nuclear decay with a half-life of 5,730 years.

In undergoing beta decay, the nucleus emits an electron from one of its neutrons, which then becomes a proton. This of course changes the atomic number, and the atom now has a new identity: nitrogen-14, the most common and stable isotope of nitrogen gas.

At first one might think that the fact there is any carbon-14 in the biosphere at all is proof of a young earth, since it should have all decayed into nitrogen in less than a million years. However, carbon-14 is being continuously produced in the upper atmosphere as cosmic rays produce free neutrons which then collide with atoms of nitrogen-14, dislodging a proton as the neutron is absorbed.

Very early in Earth's history (whether one is a creationist or an evolutionist), the amount of carbon-14 in the atmosphere would increase until the rate of its formation balances the rate of its decay – a state called *equilibrium*. An analogy would be to imagine someone trying to fill a leaky barrel with a garden hose. Eventually the incoming water would balance the outgoing water, and the water level in the barrel would remain constant.

In the 1940's, Willard Libby realized that this process could be used to date organic matter that was once part of a living organism (e.g., wood, wine, textiles, etc.). Libby's thinking involved the following assumptions:

1. After equilibrium was reached, the ratio of carbon-14 to carbon-12 in the atmosphere would be the same in all living organisms exchanging carbon with the environment.
2. The ratio of carbon-14 to carbon-12 in the atmosphere in the past was the same as it is today.
3. When an organism dies it stops exchanging carbon, and the carbon-14 sequestered in its tissues would begin to decay into nitrogen gas. The carbon-12 atoms would remain unchanged.

4. After a period of time has passed, the ratio of carbon-14 to carbon-12 in the dead tissue would become some percentage of the original ratio, and the original ratio was assumed to be the same as that of modern carbon.
5. The "percent of modern carbon" could then be applied to the 5,730-year half-life to determine how many half-lives have passed since the organism died.
6. The sensitivity limit of the testing apparatus would determine the oldest dates obtainable by this method. (The limit used to be about 50,000 years, but modern accelerator mass spectrometers can detect an individual atom of carbon-14, making the limit about 100,000 years for a typical carbon sample.)

Unfortunately, even evolutionists now realize there are numerous complications in applying Libby's method (for which he won the 1960 Nobel Prize in chemistry):

1. Libby assumed that the carbon-14 to carbon-12 ratio would reach equilibrium in the biosphere after 32,000 years, but the ratio is observed to *still be increasing*. Secular scientists realize this would imply a young age for the earth, so they have developed a "calibration curve" as a rescue device for their model.
2. There are varying levels of carbon-14 in different organisms. For example, living mollusks have been carbon dated to be 40,000 years old based on their carbon-14 content. (Scientists refer to this problem as fractionation.)
3. There are different levels of carbon-14 throughout the biosphere (reservoir effects).
4. Various phenomena can affect the carbon ratio in the biosphere. Certainly, the Flood would have buried billions of tons of carbon, isolating it from atmospheric carbon. Burning of fossil fuels and above-ground nuclear tests in the 1950's and 60's would respectively decrease or increase the levels. A stronger magnetic field in the past would have changed the "initial conditions" with less carbon-14 produced.
5. Any carbon sample older than 100,000 years should have no carbon-14 left, but tests have found measurable carbon-14 in coal samples assumed to be tens of millions of years old, and even in diamonds assumed to be at least 1 billion years old by secular scientists. Evolutionists have tried to rescue their theory by claiming sample contamination, or subsurface free neutrons acting on nitrogen atoms, but these arguments have been debunked[36]

Evidence for a Young Universe[37]

- Existence of spiral galaxies – If the universe were really billions of years old, the star arrangement the arms of spiral galaxies should have long ago "wound up".
- Existence of short-period comets – With every revolution around the sun, comets lose some of their mass. Any comet with a period of less than 200 years should have disappeared less than 20,000 years ago.
- Radiant heat from planets – The gas giants Saturn and Jupiter radiate more energy than they receive from the sun. This cannot have been going on for billions of years.

- Supernova – There are not enough supernova remnants in our galaxy to support an age more than a few thousand years, and their expansion rate implies the remnants should be much larger if they had been expanding for more than 10,000 years.

But what about the light-travel time problem?[215ff]

Critics of the Creation Model frequently point to astronomical observations that suggest that since we can see light from distant galaxies that are billions of light years away, the universe must be billions of years old to give that light time to get to us. They ignore, (or perhaps are unaware), that the Evolution Model has a light-travel problem of its own called the *horizon problem*, for which they had to concoct a rescue device involving a period of cosmic inflation during which the universe expanded faster than the speed of light. A number of creation scientists have offered theoretical explanations for the light travel problem (e.g., Humphries, Lisle, Hartnett, Setterfield, etc.), and diving into these theories would take us too far "into the weeds" for our purposes. I find Dr. Russel Humphries' explanation to be the most robust, applying Einstein's equations of general relativity, but it draws the ire of secular scientists because he assumes a bounded universe (i.e., one that would have a center, and therefore a center of mass). However, if one allows for this reasonable assumption, the outcome is that we have a universe where relativistic time dilation allows for billions of years in the outer regions, and only thousands of years near the center. This would naturally require that our Milky Way galaxy is near the center of the universe. As a creationist, I have no problem with that. For a more complete discussion, see Chapter 8 of Dr. Sarfati's book and the references therein.

Conclusion

Every week new scientific discoveries are discrediting the Evolution Model. Attempts to explain chemical evolution of life, the origin of information in DNA/RNA, stellar evolution, irreducible complexity in nature or the fine tuning of the universe have failed miserably. The notion of deep time has been shown to be false; radiometric dating requires assumptions that are not valid in the real world. Dating schemes are shown to be in conflict with each other, and in conflict with known dates. Carbon-14 dating has been shown to only be valid for dates within the last few thousand years. Evolutionists are constantly having to patch up their theory to accommodate new data.

In contrast, the Creation Model has stood unchanged for thousands of years. While scientific research has shed more light on the details of the scriptural account, the authority of the Bible is only enhanced by recent discoveries.

Brilliant creationist scientists and scholars are proving every day that one does not have to "park one's brain at the church door". In fact, it is becoming harder and harder to be an atheist in light of the continuing discoveries in science. More and more testimonies of creationist scientist are describing how the study of *science* led them to God. In fact, Francis Bacon (considered the father of the scientific method) once said, "A little science (philosophy) inclineth a man's heart to atheism, but depth in science bringeth men's minds about to religion."

For more information in the form of books, articles, professional journals, newsletters, periodicals, DVD's and podcasts, go to: www.answersingenesis.org ; www.creation.com ; www.icr.org ; www.creationresearch.org

Endnotes and References

The primary source material for these messages is from:

Sarfati, J.D. 2018. *The Genesis Account.* Creation Book Publishers, Powder Springs, GA.

Dr. Sarfati's book is "a theological, historical, and scientific commentary on Genesis 1-11", and this book can in many ways be considered a condensed version of that nearly 800-page tome. Numbers in super-scripted brackets refer to the page(s) in Dr. Sarfati's book where more information can be found. It is highly recommended that anyone who intends to use these messages for his or her own presentations read the parallel passages in *The Genesis Account* first.

1 creation.com/amazing-admissions-lewontin

2 Douglas, N.C. Lin. 2008. The Genesis of Planets. *Scientific American Magazine.* 298(5):52.

3 O"Brien, J.O., W.E. Johnson. 2007. The Evolution of Cats. *Scientific American Magazine.* 297(1):68-75.

4 Bell, P. Oldest Snake Fossils Found. 1 March 2015. creation.com. Accessed 27 Oct 2020.

5 Menton, D.M. 2012. Fearfully and Wonderfully Made (DVD). Answers in Genesis, Hebron, KY.

6 O'Micks,J. Modern Science Catches Up with Neandertal Man. Review of Papagianni, D. and M. Morse. 2015. The Neandertals Rediscovered: How Modern Science is Rewriting Their Story. *Journal of Creation* 32(1): 38-42. Accessed on creation.com.

7 Morris, H.M. 2012. *The Henry Morris Study Bible*. Master Books, Green Forest, AR. p.6.

8 Ibid. p.45.

9 Ibid. p.33.

10 Woodmorappe, J. 2003. *Noah's Ark: A Feasibility Study*. Institute for Creation Research, El Cajon, CA.

11 Morris, H.M. 2012. *The Henry Morris Study Bible*. Master Books, Green Forest, AR. p.36.

12 Bonatti, E. 2005. Earth's Mantle Below the Oceans. *Scientific American Magazine*, Special Editions 15, 2s. pp. 64-73

13 Vardiman, L. et.al. 2005. *Radioisotopes and the Age of the Earth, Vol 2.* Institute of Creation Research, El Cajon, CA.

14 Cousteau, J. 1985. *The Ocean World.* Harry N. Abrams, Inc, New York, NY. p.18.

15 Morris, H.M. 2012. *The Henry Morris Study Bible*. Master Books, Green Forest, AR. p.48.

16 Ibid. p.49.

17 Ibid. pp.43 & 49.
18 Wong, K. et. al. 2003. New Look at Human Evolution. *Scientific American Magazine*, Special Edition 13(2).
19 Jablonski, N.G. and G. Chaplin. 2003. Skin Deep. *Scientific American Magazine*, Special Edition 13(2). pp. 72-79.
20 Wong, K. 2003. Who Were the Neandertals? *Scientific American Magazine*, Special Edition 13(2). pp. 28-37.
21 Sarfati, J. 2021. Physicist Staunchly Defends Biblical Creation: Jonathan Sarfati chats with Dr. Russell Humphreys. *Creation* 43(1). p. 45
22 Snelling, A. et. al. *The New Answers Book 4.* Master Books, Green Forest, AR, Ch. 10.
23 Sarfati, J. 2004. Refuting Compromise. Master Books, Inc., Green Forest, AR. p. 365.
24 Hodge, B. 2008. How Old Is the Earth? *The New Answers Book 2*. Master Books, Green Forest, AR. Ch. 19.
25 Margenau, H. and A. Varghese. 1994. *Cosmos, Bios, Theos*. Open Court Publishing, Chicago, IL. Ch. 16.
26 Morris, H.M. 2012. *The Henry Morris Study Bible*. Master Books, Green Forest, AR. p.1869.
27 Ross, H. 1993. *The Creator and the Cosmos*. NavPress, Colorado Springs, CO. Ch. 14.
28 Brown, J. 2021. *The Leading Edge*. Blog dated 1/9/2021. Accessed from Bill Bonner's Diary, Rogue Economics, rogueeconomics.com.
29 See for example: Denton, M. 1998. *Nature's Destiny*. The Free Press, New York, NY.; Grigg, R.(ed.). 2016. *Our Amazing Created Solar System*. Creation Books Publishers; Gonzalez, G. and J. Richards. 2004. *The Privileged Planet*. Regnery Publishing.
30 See #5 above.
31 Riddle, M. *Dating Fossils and Rocks*. Microsoft PowerPoint presentation. Train2Eequip.com (now www.creationtraining.org).
32 Humphrey, D.R. 2005. *Radioisotopes and the Age of the Earth, Vol 2.* Institute of Creation Research, El Cajon, CA. Ch. 2.
33 Cupps, V. 2014. The Iconic Isochron; Radioactive Dating Part 2. *Acts & Facts*, Nov 2014. Institute for Creation Research, Dallas, TX.
34 Cupps, V. 2014. Clocks in Rocks? Radioactive Dating Part 1. *Acts & Facts*, Oct 2014. Institute for Creation Research, Dallas, TX.
35 Royal Society of Chemistry, www.rsc.org/periodic-table
36 Baumgardner, J. 2005. *Radioisotopes and the Age of the Earth, Vol 2.* Institute of Creation Research, El Cajon, CA. Ch. 8.
37 Batten, D. 2009. *Age of the Earth: 101 Evidences for a Young Age of the Earth and the Universe*. Creation Ministries International, www.creation.com . Published 4 June 2009.

ABOUT THE AUTHOR

I grew up in a small community about fifteen miles outside of Louisville, Kentucky, where I was blessed with successful and educated parents and an older brother who still shares his wisdom with me frequently. After graduating with a degree in physics from Indiana University in 1972, I served as an officer in the U.S. Air Force, mostly in South Dakota. After returning to civilian life, I started a solar energy business and later moved through a variety of professions including industrial maintenance supervision and technical sales of industrial automation equipment, while also becoming a husband and father. It was during this time that I became a Christian.

In 1995 we moved to Hilton Head Island, South Carolina, and five years later I became a science teacher at my daughter's Christian school. (Imagine being taught high school physics by your own father! Poor kid.) During my thirteen years of teaching, two things became painfully obvious to me: (1) Most people do not share my passion for pursuing scientific knowledge, and (2) most people (including Christians) have been indoctrinated into believing that the theory of evolution disproves the Bible (largely a result of (1) above).

I had always integrated biblical truth into my teaching, but since I only taught physical science, evolutionary theory was not in the scope of my lessons as it would be for a teacher of life science or Earth science. It so happened I was tasked to develop a curriculum for environmental science, and that textbook contained the obligatory genuflection to evolutionary theory, which I ultimately developed into a full unit of instruction. That's right – I was teaching evolution, but in a private school a teacher can point out the scientific challenges confronting the theory, and even propose alternative theories such as intelligent design or even biblical creation. My goal was not to *indoctrinate* my students, but to develop within them the ability to think critically, examine competing explanations, evaluate arguments and arrive at the superior scientific model to explain the evidence we observe in the world around us.

I saw some successes with students who went on to college and told me they were able to defend their faith in a secular environment with the foundation they had been given in my class. But I was only able to work with a small fraction of all the students that my school graduated, which was in turn a tinier fraction of all students in my community. I realized that many more young people could be reached through their church pastors and youth leaders, but sadly these well-meaning Christians were not equipped to counter the indoctrination that students were receiving in school, movies, TV shows and the Internet. That was my motivation in writing *Genesis Analysis for Pastors*. My goal is that any pastor, youth leader, Bible study facilitator or parent can use these canned presentations in a verse-by-verse exposition of the first eleven chapters of the book of Genesis (the portion of the Bible that most directly confronts evolutionary theory).

Even the most casual observer will note there is no "Ph.D" after my name, and I don't claim to be an authority about anything. However, the authors and writers that I reference in this book *are* credentialled authorities in their respective fields. I have been avidly researching the creation/evolution debate for over thirty years, and trust me, I have heard every argument and counter-argument there is for either world view.

My prayer is that this book will encourage everyone who reads it to boldly proclaim the authority of the Bible in all aspects of the human experience, but especially in the areas of science that the Bible touches on. The Bible does not claim to be a science textbook, which is a good thing since science textbooks are revised every few years in order to stay factually correct and up to date. The Bible, on the other hand, was inerrant in its original autographs, and remains inerrant when correctly translated to this day. My daughter's university physics text was in its 11th edition when she was in college, and the copy I had from an AP physics curriculum was a 9th edition, but the Bibles in print today are still being translated from the "first edition". (Yes, that's right; my daughter took physics in college, as well. Or should I say it took her!)

Please adapt these messages to your own needs and presentation style. Digital versions are available in Microsoft Word™ or PDF format so that you can cut-and-paste or edit as you choose. Microsoft PowerPoint™ slides to accompany each message are also available. Simply ask by using the contact information in the section entitled "How to Contact the Author".

In His service,

Richard Sanders

http://genesisanalysis.com

www.ingramcontent.com/pod-product-compliance
Ingram Content Group UK Ltd.
Pitfield, Milton Keynes, MK11 3LW, UK
UKHW061706190726
13853UKWH00008B/2434

9 798718 448283